delish

275+ AMAZING RECIPES & IDEAS!

delish

Joanna Saltz & The Editors of Delish

HOUGHTON MIFFLIN HARCOURT

Boston   New York

TO THE PEOPLE WHO ARE ALWAYS DAYDREAMING ABOUT THEIR NEXT MEAL:
WE SEE YOU.

For information about permission to reproduce selections from this book, write to trade.permissions@hmhco.com or to Permissions, Houghton Mifflin Harcourt Publishing Company, 3 Park Avenue, 19th Floor, New York, New York 10016.

hmhbooks.com

Library of Congress Cataloging-in-Publication Data is available.
ISBN 978-1-328-49886-1 (hbk)
ISBN 978-1-328-49946-2 (ebk)
ISBN 978-0-358-68236-3 (pbk)

Book design by Laura Palese

Art direction and illustrations by Delish

Printed in China

SCP 10 9 8 7 6 5 4 3 2 1

CONTENTS

7
CARB YOUR ENTHUSIASM
183

8
TEX-MEX MADNESS
213

9
GOOD FOR YOU!
243

10
BRUNCH TIME
275

11
THERE'S ALWAYS ROOM . . .
317

12
FRIENDSGIVING & MORE
367

INTRODUCTION

You don't have to know how to cook— you just have to love to eat.

THE DELISH 15 IS REAL. It's the 15 pounds that you gain when you first start working here—kind of like the first few weeks of college. It happens because every day at around 4 p.m. something bananas comes out of the test kitchen: a gigantic pot of Chicken Parm soup, a tray of Jell-O shots, a whole salmon . . . it's a mixed bag. And every day, we gather around, push each other out of the way to get a taste, and have a bitch session. "Why am I eating this whole thing? I just had lunch." "I promised myself no added sugars this month." "I don't even LIKE peanut butter but I can't stop myself."

Restraint is hard when you're producing recipes at the rate we do. And no matter how good you're trying to be, something is going to strike your fancy. This is why 1) I sneak out to go to the gym every day in the late morning, and 2) Lauren Miyashiro, our senior food editor, came

Our first appearance on *Good Morning America*

up with the two-bite rule: You get two bites of any food and then you're done. These are our defense mechanisms, as futile as they might be.

It wasn't always this way at Delish. When we took over the brand three and a half years ago, there were five of us total, and we made one—maybe two—recipes a week. Don't get me wrong; they were super-fun recipes and we look back on them longingly (our Tuscan Chicken Pasta on page 185 is OG Delish and still one of our favorites). But Lindsay Funston, our deputy editor and my very first hire, would style her food on the hallway floor near a daylight window and take photos on her phone. We would turn up Drake in our little test kitchen,

Summer party at the Jersey shore

beg the people in our office building to come in for a bite, and bring food to anyone we had a meeting with. We were so excited for people to know who we were and what we were trying to build.

It was all in the name of carving out our own niche in the food universe. We wanted to create a place for someone who, we imagined, loved to eat more than he or she loved to cook. Maybe she didn't feel totally comfortable in the kitchen; maybe he was completely happy eating Chipotle every night. (Trust us: We've been there.) We thought that if our kitchen felt fun in real life—if Delish was an actual place filled with amazing food and tons of laughs where people wanted to hang out—that feeling would carry over to the rest of the world.

Fast-forward to now: The staff is bigger, the food is shot on actual surfaces with real cameras, the offices are a little fancier—but the only thing that hasn't changed is that feeling. We laugh loud and eat well and sing obnoxiously . . . and we bring our food to every meeting. And we still believe that no one should be afraid to get into the kitchen, and that a great recipe can actually start a party.

That's really what we mean when we say, "Eat like every day's the weekend." There's a relaxedness to how we all cook on Saturdays and Sundays—and having people over can mean anything from a sit-down dinner around slow-cooker carnitas (page 220) to cupcakes and cocktails in front of the TV. There's no pressure to be perfect, no fear about failure, and food just seems to taste better when you're shoving friends and family out of the way to eat it. But we think that feeling can happen any time of the week—whether it's dinner on a busy Thursday night or a snack at the office on Tuesday afternoon. You just need ideas that are as fun to make as they are to eat.

To be honest, the hardest part about creating this cookbook has been trimming down the recipe list to fit within the 386 pages here: There were so many things we wanted to show you. And every corner of the book is crammed not just with delicious food, but also with the helpful tips, weird tricks, and crazy stories we picked up along our insane journey.

So hopefully, by the time you've reached the end of this book, you'll have flagged three recipes and texted at least one friend about what you're going to make together. Then we'll feel like we've done our job.

JOANNA SALTZ
Editorial Director

NYC subway family photo

The best kitchen team ever ⊢——→

MEET TEA

**JOANNA SALTZ,
AKA "JO"**

Editorial Director

"Do you trust me?"

**LINDSAY FUNSTON,
AKA "FUNS"**

Deputy Editor

*"Started from the bottom,
now we here."*

NICK NEUBECK

Creative Director

"Can we raccoon this up?"

**LINDSEY RAMSEY,
AKA "RAMS"**

Managing Editor

"Did ANYONE read my email?"

LAUREN MIYASHIRO

Senior Food Editor

"How can we super-size this?"

LENA ABRAHAM

Assistant Food Editor

"In Funs we trust."

M DELISH

**PHILIP B. SWIFT,
AKA "HAMZAMMER"**

Senior Video Producer

*"Dissin' headlines and missin'
deadlines since 2016."*

**CANDACE BRAUN
DAVISON**

Senior Editor

"Sure, I'll try it."

CHELSEA LUPKIN

Creative Video Producer

*"I need someone to open this
avocado."*

VINEET SAWANT

Video Editor

"Eat or be eaten."

SARAH WEINBERG

Senior Features Editor/Unofficial
Bachelor Correspondent

*"The higher the cheese pull, the
closer to God."*

JULIA SMITH

Associate Social Media Editor

"Carbin' not starvin'."

CONTINUES ➔

EAT LIKE NO ONE

WILL EVER SEE YOU NAKED

SAMANTHA NETKIN

Assistant Social Media Editor

"That's too spicy."

BRANDON BALES

Video Editor

"Mayonnaise-colored Benz, we push Miracle Whips."

ALEX MUSTO

Video Editor

"I don't think I have a motto."

ZACHARY LENNON-SIMON

Video Editor

"Pizza."

SIENNA FANTOZZI

Assistant Editor

"It's done."

ALLIE FOLINO

Designer

"Eat your spaghetti to forgetti your regretti."

ETHAN CALABRESE, AKA "IAN CALAMARI"

Photographer

"Dead dove. Do not eat."

MAKINZE GORE

Food Assistant

"When buying cream cheese and bacon, always double the amount and pray it's enough."

TESS KOMAN

Features Editor

"Under her (Ina's) eye."

MADDIE FLAGER

Assistant Editor

"Is there an embargo on that?"

welcome to boozetown

CHAPTER ONE

BUT FIRST, DRINKS!

GIGGLE JUICE

Seems fitting to start this book off with a laugh. WTF is Giggle Juice, you ask? We fell in love with the name after Candace spotted it on a restaurant menu. Kind of besides the point, honestly: The quirky combo of pink lemonade, moscato, and vodka will definitely make you LOL.

Lemon wedge, for rimming glasses

Sugar, for rimming glasses

1 (750-ml) bottle moscato

3 cups pink lemonade

1 can lemon-lime soda

1 cup vodka

2 cups sliced strawberries

1 lemon, sliced into half-moons

Ice

1. Rim glasses with lemon wedge and dip in sugar.

2. In a large pitcher, stir together moscato, pink lemonade, soda, vodka, and fruit. Add ice and stir to combine.

3. Divide among glasses and serve.

PROSECCO GRAPES

TOTAL TIME: 1 HR 10 MIN / SERVES 10

Drunken fruit is our favorite way to party: You soak grapes
in prosecco and vodka until they're totally infused, then roll them
in sugar and throw them back.

2 pounds green grapes

1 (750-ml) bottle prosecco

4 ounces vodka

½ cup sugar

1. In a large bowl, pour prosecco and vodka over grapes. Let soak in fridge at least 1 hour.

2. Drain grapes in a colander and pat dry, then transfer to a small baking sheet and pour sugar on top. Shake pan back and forth until grapes are fully coated in sugar.

3. Serve in a bowl.

 Follow this same technique for boozy **STRAWBERRIES, WATERMELON,** and **PINEAPPLE.**

We don't usually love unitasking kitchen gadgets, but we love a **PINEAPPLE CORER.** Whole pineapples cost way less than cored, and this tool hollows one in 45 seconds flat.

PINEAPPLE COLADAS

TOTAL TIME: 15 MIN / MAKES 2

If you like piña coladas . . . yeah yeah, you need these. Because nothing is more fun than drinking something out of a pineapple (seriously—it's the best cure for transporting yourself to a happier place in the middle of February).

2 pineapples, tops sliced off

4 ounces light rum

1 ounce dark rum

4 ounces coconut cream

Splash of pineapple juice

Splash of coconut milk

Ice

1. Using a pineapple corer, remove top ¾ of inside pineapples. (Be careful not to pierce through bottom of pineapple—your drinks will leak!) Use a knife to carefully remove remaining core; discard.

2. Chop one cored pineapple into large chunks and add to a blender with light and dark rums, coconut cream, pineapple juice, and coconut milk. (Reserve second cored pineapple for later use.) Fill blender with ice and blend until slushy.

3. Pour drinks into cored pineapples and top with a paper umbrella.

5 WAYS TO MAKE MARGARITAS

Welcome to Margaritaville. Population: You.

1 CREAMSICLE

Blend 1½ cups orange juice, ½ cup lime juice, ½ cup tequila, and ¼ cup triple sec with ice. Rim four glasses with an orange wedge and dip in sugar. Fill each glass with margarita mixture. Dollop with Cool Whip and garnish with an orange slice and zest.

2 BLUE CRUSH

In a pitcher, stir together 4 cups seltzer, 1 cup tequila, ⅔ cup lime juice, ½ cup each blue curaçao and triple sec, and ice. Rim four glasses with a lime wedge and dip in salt. Fill each glass with ice and margarita mixture. Garnish with lime.

3 APPLE CIDER

In a pitcher, stir together 3 cups apple cider, 1 cup tequila, and ¼ cup lemon juice. Dip four glasses in water, then a mixture of sugar, cinnamon, and salt. Fill each glass with ice and margarita mixture. Garnish with an apple slice and cinnamon stick.

4 PINK LEMONADE

In a pitcher, stir together 3 cups pink lemonade, 1 cup tequila, ¼ cup lemon juice, and ¼ cup triple sec. Rim four glasses with a lemon wedge and dip in salt. Fill each glass with ice and margarita mixture. Garnish with lemon.

5 BULLDOG

Blend 1 cup tequila, ⅔ cup lime juice, ¼ cup triple sec, and ¼ cup sugar with ice. Rim four glasses with a lime wedge and dip in salt. Fill each glass with margarita mixture. Pop caps of 4 Coronitas and flip each upside down into a glass. Garnish with lime.

CREAMSICLE
MARGARITA

WTF?

TIKI TREASURE CHEST

THREE DOTS AND A DASH / Chicago, IL

When it comes to tiki drinks, over-the-top is the norm: If they're not flaming or garnished with enough tropical fruit to feed a family of four, they're not worth your time. But no bar goes as extreme as Three Dots and a Dash in Chicago, which serves a $385 Treasure Chest of booze hidden beneath a dry ice–induced cloud of smoke. The cocktail is a mix of guava, pineapple, and orange juice, plus some fresh lime, pomegranate syrup, and rum. It's so massive, the concoction is mixed in a glass skull the size of a mixing bowl and poured into a treasure chest the size of a bassinet. Then, to add a little fizz, the whole thing's topped with an entire bottle of Dom Pérignon—hence that jaw-dropping price tag.

MARGARITA SLUSHY SHOTS

TOTAL TIME: 10 MIN / MAKES 4

These might pack a punch, but they won't bring you back to that night of too many tequila shots. You blend up a super-simple frozen marg mixture, pour it over chopped fruit, and then say "Cheers!"

6 ounces silver tequila

**Juice of 3 limes
(1 rind reserved)**

2 tablespoons honey

1 cup ice

**Coarse or margarita salt,
for rimming glasses**

**Chopped strawberries,
pineapple, blackberries,
and raspberries, for shots**

1. In a blender, combine tequila, lime juice, honey, and ice and blend until slushy.

2. Rim four shot glasses with a juiced lime and dip in salt.

3. Fill shot glasses with chopped fruit and margarita mixture.

POT O' GOLD SHOTS

TOTAL TIME: 2 HRS 10 MIN / MAKES 16

At most bars, St. Patrick's Day means green beer. We thought it was time to break tradition with these so-kitschy-cute-it's-almost-annoying Jell-O shots. Using sour candy belts as rainbows is a must; you can find them at any candy store. It's your lucky day.

1 (3.4-ounce) package lemon or pineapple Jell-O

½ cup cold whiskey

1 cup Cool Whip

Gold sprinkles

6 rainbow candy belts, cut into 2-inch pieces

1. In a small saucepan, bring 1 cup water to a boil. Add Jell-O mix and stir until dissolved. Turn off heat and stir in ½ cup more water and the whiskey. Place 16 plastic shot glasses on a baking sheet and pour in mixture until each is two-thirds full.

2. Refrigerate until set, about 2 hours.

3. Top each with a dollop of Cool Whip and gold sprinkles. Place a rainbow candy belt on top, forming it into a semicircle like a rainbow, before serving.

THIS GRANDMA IS A BEER PONG CHAMPION

When Pauline Kana introduces herself, it's as Granny. Never mind the fact that you're not related to her: It's more of a stage name for the ninety-one-year-old beer pong player. Kana is a bonafide Internet sensation thanks to her grandson-turned-teammate Ross Smith. His Instagram account, @smoothsmith8, is filled with short videos of her shooting—and scoring—trick shot after trick shot: out of a car window, from the top of a staircase, off a frying pan. If it were up to Kana, though, their beer cups would be filled with something a little stronger. "Margaritas are my drink," she says.

Before pong, a different ball was life: Granny skyrocketed to fame on Vine after Smith posted a six-second clip of Kana playing basketball. Since then, the duo's dabbled in every sport, and they've documented all of it for their fans on social media. The gig's gotten Kana so much attention, it's nearly taken her out of retirement: She and Smith earned an invite to the 2017 World Series of Beer Pong in Las Vegas, a four-day tournament of epically sloppy proportions.

The granny-grandson team's reputation is more trick than triumph, so Granny's skills translate better in a highlight reel than a competition: They didn't take down the 250 other teams—not even close—but Kana is still a baller in her grandson's eyes. "She's way more clutch than I am," Smith boasts. "She's got ice in her veins."

SHARK ATTACK SHOTS

TOTAL TIME: 1 HR 10 MIN / MAKES 12

Everyone knows the best TV to watch in July is Shark Week—and we were totally inspired to make these Jell-O shots in honor of it. A drop of red food coloring gives them their grisly, bloody look.

1 (3.4-ounce) package blue Jell-O

1 cup boiling water

1 cup light rum

12 gummy sharks

Red food coloring

1. In a 2-cup liquid measuring cup, whisk together Jell-O mix, boiling water, and rum.

2. Place a gummy shark in each of 12 plastic shot glasses. Place glasses on a baking sheet and fill with Jell-O mixture Ⓐ. Refrigerate 20 minutes Ⓑ.

3. Add a drop of red food coloring to each glass Ⓒ and swirl with a toothpick. Refrigerate until completely firm, 40 minutes more.

WATCH & LEARN

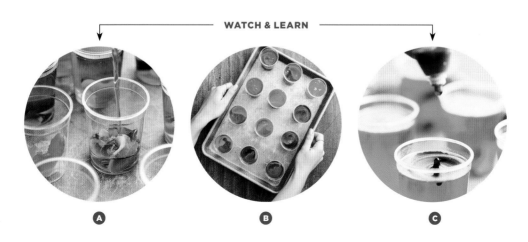

Ⓐ   Ⓑ   Ⓒ

MERMAID LEMONADE

TOTAL TIME: 10 MIN / SERVES 4

For anyone who's dreamed of being Ariel (so . . . all of us?!), this cocktail's for you. Getting the layered ombré look is simple, but go easy with the blue curaçao—too much, and the entire drink will turn dark blue.

2 cups ice

¼ cup blue curaçao

1 cup white rum

2 cups lemonade

4 lemon slices

8 maraschino cherries

1. Put ¼ cup ice in each glass, then add a splash of blue curaçao, ¼ cup rum, and another ¼ cup ice. (The ice helps with the ombré.) Pour over ½ cup lemonade.

2. Skewer a lemon slice and 2 maraschino cherries on a paper umbrella or toothpick and garnish drinks before serving.

CARAMEL APPLE SHOTS

TOTAL TIME: 4 HRS 25 MIN / MAKES 40

There's no better way to celebrate fall than with these apple cider–spiked Jell-O shots. This hack of hollowing out apples will make your friends say, "You fancy!"

5 Granny Smith apples, halved lengthwise, stems removed

Juice of 3 lemons

1¾ cups apple cider

2 (.25-ounce) envelopes unflavored powdered gelatin

¼ cup soft caramels, melted

1 cup caramel vodka

1. Use a melon baller or teaspoon to hollow out apples, leaving a ¼" border. Brush cut surfaces with lemon juice. Place each hollow-side up in a muffin tin.

2. Pour apple cider into a small saucepan and sprinkle with gelatin; let bloom 2 minutes. (You'll notice a shimmery, ripply film on top of cider.) Whisk over low heat until gelatin has dissolved, then whisk in melted caramels. Remove from heat and stir in vodka.

3. Carefully pour mixture into hollowed-out apples.

4. Refrigerate until firm, at least 4 hours.

5. Place apples gelatin-side down on a cutting board and slice into 4 wedges each before serving.

Don't be afraid to use a little **ELBOW GREASE** when hollowing out the apples. They're tough to the core.

SANGRIA POPS

TOTAL TIME: 3 HRS 15 MIN / MAKES 14

After making pops using this Dixie cup technique, we don't know how we'll ever go back to molds. Loaded with strawberries, raspberries, and peaches (but you can really use whatever fruit you want) and spiked with white wine, these are SO refreshing.

2 cups white wine

1 cup white grape juice

½ orange, sliced into wedges, rind removed

½ cup diced peaches

¼ cup strawberries, diced

¼ cup raspberries

1

In a 3- or 4-cup liquid measuring cup, whisk together wine and grape juice until combined.

2

Place 14 paper cups on a large baking sheet. Divide fruit among each and fill with wine mixture.

3

Cover each cup with a small square of aluminum foil. Using a knife, cut a slit in the middle and insert a wooden ice cream spoon into each.

4

Freeze until firm, 3 hours. When ready to serve, snip the rim of each cup and peel cups off pops.

"

Funston and I were trying to make these pops in the middle of July in a very hot kitchen. We created an intense assembly line and started running them to the freezer as fast as we possibly could. —**MAKINZE**

CHAPTER TWO

PARTY STARTERS

These apps & bites make hosting less annoying.

SHRIMP TOSTADA BITES

TOTAL TIME: 50 MIN / SERVES 8

If it were up to us, chips and guac would make an appearance at literally every party. This is the twist that makes it fancy enough for even the classiest gathering.

FOR THE SHRIMP

⅓ cup extra-virgin olive oil

Juice of 3 limes

2 tablespoons honey

2 cloves garlic, minced

1 teaspoon paprika

¼ teaspoon cayenne pepper

Kosher salt

1 pound peeled and deveined medium shrimp, thawed if frozen

FOR THE GUAC

2 avocados

Juice of 2 limes

½ red onion, finely chopped

½ jalapeño, finely chopped

2 tablespoons freshly chopped cilantro

Kosher salt

Tortilla scoops, for serving

1. Make shrimp: In a large bowl, whisk together olive oil, lime juice, honey, garlic, paprika, and cayenne and season with salt. Add shrimp and toss until fully coated, then cover and let marinate in fridge at least 30 minutes and up to 2 hours.

2. In a large skillet over medium heat, cook shrimp until pink and completely opaque, 2 minutes per side.

3. Make guac: In a medium bowl, mash avocados with lime juice, red onion, jalapeño, and cilantro and season generously with salt.

4. Dollop a tablespoon of guac into tortilla scoops, top with shrimp, and garnish with cilantro before serving.

GRILLED CHEESE DIPPERS

DELISH FAVE

TOTAL TIME: 45 MIN / SERVES 4

These dippers turn a regular grilled cheese (our spirit food, BTW) into a thing of magic. Plus, did you realize it was this easy to make tomato soup?!

3 tablespoons butter, divided

1 medium onion, diced

1 clove garlic, minced

1 (28-ounce) can crushed tomatoes

3 cups low-sodium chicken (or vegetable) broth

Kosher salt

Freshly ground black pepper

¼ cup heavy cream

Thinly sliced fresh basil, for garnish

8 slices white bread, crusts removed

8 slices cheddar cheese

1. In a large pot over medium heat, melt 1 tablespoon butter. Add onion and cook until beginning to soften, 2 to 3 minutes. Stir in garlic and cook until fragrant, 1 minute more.

2. Add crushed tomatoes and broth and season generously with salt and pepper. Bring to a boil, then reduce heat and simmer 15 minutes. Stir in heavy cream and top with basil.

3. Using a rolling pin, roll bread into flat, ¼-inch-thick squares **A**. Place 1 slice cheddar cheese on each piece of bread **B** and tightly roll up **C**.

4. In a large nonstick skillet over medium heat, melt 1 tablespoon butter. Working in batches, add dippers to skillet, seam-side down, and cook, turning often, until bread is golden and cheese is melty, about 3 minutes **D**. Wipe skillet clean with a paper towel and add 1 tablespoon more butter before next batch of dippers.

5. Ladle soup into bowls and serve with grilled cheese dippers.

WATCH & LEARN

A **B** **C** **D**

BUNLESS BURGER BITES

TOTAL TIME: 25 MIN / MAKES 20

You don't have to be on carb patrol to make these (but your dieting friends will love you for it). You basically make burger meatballs and then skewer them with your favorite toppings.

1 pound ground beef

½ cup plain breadcrumbs

1 large egg

2 cloves garlic, minced

1 tablespoon Worcestershire sauce

1 tablespoon yellow mustard

Kosher salt

Freshly ground black pepper

1 tablespoon vegetable oil

5 slices cheddar cheese, quartered

6 leaves Bibb lettuce, torn into large pieces

1 small jar dill pickle chips

1 pint cherry tomatoes

1. In a large bowl, combine ground beef, breadcrumbs, egg, garlic, Worcestershire, and mustard and season with salt and pepper. Mix until fully combined, then form into small, meatball-size patties.

2. In a large skillet over medium heat, heat oil. Cook patties until your desired doneness, 6 to 8 minutes per side for medium.

3. Top each with a cheese square and cover with lid to let melt, 2 minutes.

4. Thread a patty, lettuce, pickle, and tomato on each appetizer skewer and serve.

JALAPEÑO POPPER WONTON CUPS

TOTAL TIME: 30 MIN / MAKES 12

There is nothing in the world that the Delish kitchen hasn't jalapeño-poppered. Whether as a dip, grilled cheese, egg rolls, stuffed chicken (there's more . . . believe us), the bacon–cream cheese–jalapeño combo is our obsession.

Cooking spray

12 wonton wrappers

8 slices bacon

1 (8-ounce) block cream cheese, softened

¼ cup sour cream

1 teaspoon garlic powder

Kosher salt

Freshly ground black pepper

1 cup shredded cheddar cheese

1 cup shredded Monterey jack cheese

2 jalapeños, finely chopped

1. Preheat oven to 350°F and grease a muffin tin with cooking spray. Place a wonton wrapper into each muffin tin cup and bake until lightly golden, about 8 minutes.

2. In a large nonstick skillet, cook bacon until crispy, 8 minutes. Drain on a paper towel-lined plate, then chop.

3. Meanwhile, in a medium bowl, stir together cream cheese, sour cream, and garlic powder until combined and season with salt and pepper. Fold in ¾ cup each cheddar cheese and Monterey jack cheese, most of the bacon, and jalapeños.

4. Spoon a heaping tablespoon of jalapeño popper mixture into each wonton cup and top with remaining cheeses and bacon.

5. Bake until wontons are deeply golden and cheese is melty, about 8 minutes more.

STEAK FRITE BITES

TOTAL TIME: 50 MIN / SERVES 6 TO 8

We've had feelings for these since someone dreamed them up during a brainstorm: strips of flank steak wrapped around French fries and drizzled with your favorite steak sauce. A genius twist on the classic French dinner.

1 pound flank steak, pounded ¼ inch thick

2 tablespoons extra-virgin olive oil

1 tablespoon freshly chopped rosemary

1 tablespoon Dijon mustard

2 tablespoons Worcestershire sauce

Kosher salt

Freshly ground black pepper

½ (1-pound) bag frozen French fries

Vegetable oil, for grill

Steak sauce, for serving

1. Preheat oven according to French fry package directions. Slice steak against the grain, on the diagonal, into thin 2-inch-long strips.

2. In a large bowl, whisk together olive oil, rosemary, Dijon, and Worcestershire, then add steak and toss to coat. Let marinate in the fridge, at least 15 minutes and up to 2 hours. When ready to grill, generously season with salt and pepper.

3. Meanwhile, bake frozen fries according to package directions. Let cool slightly.

4. Heat a grill to medium-high or heat a grill pan over medium-high heat. Grease grates or pan with vegetable oil. Place four to five baked French fries on top of a piece of steak and roll up; secure with a toothpick. Repeat until all steak and fries are used up.

5. Grill until charred, about 2 minutes per side for medium-rare.

6. Drizzle with steak sauce before serving.

BUFFACUE WINGS

TOTAL TIME: 1 HR 10 MIN / SERVES 8 TO 10

Our staff is deeply divided on the important issues: blue cheese or ranch; cheddar or American; Buffalo or barbecue. This is our bipartisan approach to wings. It's super tangy and pretty spicy, but also pleases everyone.

2 pounds chicken wings

2 tablespoons extra-virgin olive oil

2 teaspoons garlic powder, divided

Kosher salt

Freshly ground black pepper

½ cup Buffalo sauce

¼ cup barbecue sauce

2 tablespoons butter

2 tablespoons honey

1. Preheat oven to 400°F and place a wire rack over a large baking sheet.

2. In a large bowl, toss chicken wings with oil and season with 1 teaspoon garlic powder, salt, and pepper. Transfer to prepared baking sheet.

3. Bake, flipping wings halfway through, until golden and crispy, 50 to 60 minutes. Transfer to a large bowl. Switch oven to broil.

4. Meanwhile, in a small saucepan over low heat, whisk together Buffalo and barbecue sauces, butter, honey, and remaining 1 teaspoon garlic powder. Bring to a simmer, then remove from heat.

5. Pour sauce over wings, tossing to combine. Return wings to baking sheet and broil until caramelized, 2 to 3 minutes.

5 WAYS TO MAKE NACHOS

If you're not in the mood for nachos,
you can't sit with us.

1 PHILLY CHEESESTEAK

In a large skillet over medium heat, heat 1 tablespoon vegetable oil. Add 1 sliced onion and 2 sliced bell peppers and season with salt and pepper. Cook until soft, then push to one side of skillet and add another tablespoon oil and 1 pound thinly sliced sirloin in a single layer. Season with 1 teaspoon Italian seasoning, salt, and pepper. Sear, then stir together with onions and peppers and cook 3 minutes more. On a foil-lined baking sheet, layer one (18-ounce) bag tortilla chips and top with 2 cups shredded provolone cheese, 1 cup shredded mozzarella, and the steak and peppers. Bake at 400°F for 15 minutes.

2 GREEK

Slice 6 pitas into wedges and place in a single layer on a foil-lined baking sheet. Drizzle with 2 tablespoons olive oil and season with 1 teaspoon oregano, salt, and pepper; toss to combine. Bake at 400°F until golden, 10 minutes. In a large bowl, combine ¾ cup crumbled feta cheese, ¼ cup Greek yogurt, ¼ cup olive oil, and juice of ½ lemon and beat with a hand mixer until fluffy. Dollop whipped feta cheese over baked pita and top with ½ cup each chopped cucumber, kalamata olives, and cherry tomatoes. Sprinkle with fresh dill, drizzle with olive oil, and squeeze with lemon.

3 DORITOS CHICKEN

Mix 2 cups nacho cheese with one (15-ounce) can drained Rotel. On a foil-lined baking sheet, layer one (15-ounce) bag Nacho Cheese Doritos, 2 cups shredded rotisserie chicken, and the nacho cheese mixture. Repeat. Bake at 400°F for 10 minutes, then garnish with chopped parsley.

4 MEXICAN STREET CORN

On a foil-lined baking sheet, layer one (18-ounce) bag tortilla chips, one (15-ounce) can drained fire-roasted corn, and 3 cups shredded mozzarella. Bake at 400°F for 15 minutes. Mix ½ cup sour cream, 2 tablespoons mayonnaise, juice of ½ lime, and 1 teaspoon chili powder and drizzle over nachos. Garnish with cilantro and crumbled cotija.

5 PULLED PORK

On a foil-lined baking sheet, layer one (18-ounce) bag tortilla chips, ½ pound barbecue pulled pork, and 2 cups shredded pepper jack cheese. Repeat. Bake at 400°F for 15 minutes. Garnish with 1 cup each pickled red onions, coleslaw, and pickle chips.

PHILLY CHEESESTEAK NACHOS

SLOPPY JOE POTATO SKINS

A classic kid favorite made for grown-ups. Or kids pretending to be grown-ups. There's something about the sweet 'n' tangy flavor that kills us—and spooned over potato skins and topped with cheddar, it's even more deadly.

---

8 small russet potatoes

¼ cup extra-virgin olive oil, divided

Kosher salt

1 small onion, chopped

2 cloves garlic, minced

1½ pounds ground beef

¾ cup ketchup

¼ cup packed brown sugar

2 tablespoons Dijon mustard

1 tablespoon Worcestershire sauce

1 tablespoon chili powder

Freshly ground black pepper

1½ cups shredded cheddar cheese

Freshly chopped chives, for garnish

1. Preheat oven to 400°F.

2. Pierce potatoes all over with a fork. Place on a large baking sheet, drizzle with 1 tablespoon oil, season with salt, and toss to coat.

3. Bake until potatoes are tender and skin is crispy, 50 minutes to 1 hour. Let cool 10 minutes.

4. Meanwhile, in a large skillet over medium heat, heat 1 tablespoon oil. Add onion and cook, stirring, until soft, about 5 minutes. Stir in garlic and cook until fragrant, 1 minute more. Add ground beef and cook, breaking up the meat with a wooden spoon, until no longer pink, 6 to 8 minutes. Drain fat.

5. Return beef mixture to skillet over medium heat and stir in ketchup, brown sugar, Dijon, Worcestershire, and chili powder. Season generously with salt and pepper. Simmer until beginning to thicken, about 3 minutes, then remove from heat.

6. Halve potatoes lengthwise and carefully scoop out insides, leaving about ¼-inch-thick border. Brush insides with remaining 2 tablespoons oil and season with salt and pepper. Spoon sloppy joe mixture into each and top with cheddar cheese.

7. Return potatoes to baking sheet and bake until cheese is melty and potato skins are crispy, about 10 minutes.

8. Garnish with chives before serving.

 Save the **SCRAPED POTATOES!** They're perfect for mashed potatoes, hash browns, or soup.

WTF?

SMOKED MOZZARELLA

BARANO / Williamsburg, Brooklyn

Cheese like this is that of legend—so, we needed to see it for ourselves. Chef Al Di Meglio opened Barano on a waterfront stretch in Williamsburg, Brooklyn, with one noble effort in mind: to put mozzarella back in the spotlight. "No one focuses solely on mozzarella," he says. "It's always part of something else." That's true at Barano, too: The house-made mozz is served every which way—but the best way is all by itself. It comes to the table under a glass cloche that gets pumped with smoke in the kitchen. When it's delivered to guests—seventy times a night during a busy weekend—and the smoke pours out onto the table, heads definitely turn. His chefs make the mozz to order, which he insists sets his apart from the rest. Says Di Meglio, "When it comes out all hot and melty, there's nothing better."

REUBEN EGG ROLLS

TOTAL TIME: 40 MIN / MAKES 16

We've stuffed some crazy crap into egg rolls—cheesecake, pickles, Thanksgiving leftovers—but this New York deli twist of corned beef, sauerkraut, and Swiss is our fave.

½ **(8-ounce) block cream cheese, softened**

3 tablespoons Russian dressing, plus more for serving

1 tablespoon prepared horseradish

¾ **pound sliced corned beef, chopped**

1½ **cups shredded Swiss cheese**

½ **cup sauerkraut, drained**

2 tablespoons freshly chopped chives

16 egg roll wrappers

Vegetable oil, for frying

1. In a medium bowl, mix together cream cheese, Russian dressing, and horseradish. Fold in corned beef, Swiss, sauerkraut, and chives.

2. Set an egg roll wrapper in a diamond shape in front of you and spoon 2 tablespoons (max) reuben mixture in the center. Fold up bottom half and sides, then gently roll, sealing seam with a couple drops water. Repeat with remaining filling and wrappers.

3. In a large deep-sided skillet over medium heat, heat 1 inch oil until it starts to bubble, then, working in batches, add egg rolls and fry until golden, 1 minute per side. Drain on a paper towel–lined plate and let cool slightly. Repeat with remaining egg rolls.

4. Serve warm, with Russian dressing for dipping.

Frying egg rolls can **SOUND INTIMIDATING,** but it's definitely worth it here. The high heat keeps the wrapper crispy and prevents the whole thing from exploding.

FRENCH DIP SLIDERS

TOTAL TIME: 45 MIN / MAKES 12

This recipe is one of those shape-shifters—perfect for any occasion, from a fancy New Years cocktail party to a low-key game day. People will bow down after their first dunk in the au jus.

5 tablespoons butter, divided

1 large onion, thinly sliced

2 sprigs plus ¼ teaspoon fresh thyme

Kosher salt

Freshly ground black pepper

12 slider buns, halved

1 pound thinly sliced deli roast beef

12 slices provolone cheese

¼ teaspoon garlic powder

1 tablespoon freshly chopped parsley

1 clove garlic, minced

1½ cups low-sodium beef broth

1 tablespoon Worcestershire sauce

1. Preheat oven to 350°F.

2. In a large skillet over medium-high heat, melt 2 tablespoons butter. Add onion and thyme sprigs and season with salt and pepper. Cook, stirring occasionally, until caramelized, about 15 minutes. Discard thyme.

3. Place bottom halves of slider buns on a large baking sheet and top with roast beef, provolone cheese, caramelized onions, and slider bun tops.

4. Melt 2 tablespoons butter and brush on top of buns. Sprinkle with garlic powder, coarse salt, and parsley and bake until cheese is melty and sliders are warmed through, 10 to 15 minutes.

5. Meanwhile, make au jus: Add remaining 1 tablespoon butter to same skillet and melt over medium heat. Add garlic and cook until fragrant, 1 minute, then add beef broth, Worcestershire, and thyme and season with salt and pepper. Simmer until slightly reduced, 10 minutes.

6. Serve sliders with au jus for dipping.

SPINACH ARTICHOKE PRETZELS

TOTAL TIME: 2 HRS 30 MIN / MAKES 18

We hate fussy crap in the Delish kitchen, but pretzeling is really worth it. A super-fast dunk in a baking soda bath transforms these beauties into something amazing.

Cooking spray

¾ (8-ounce) block cream cheese, softened

⅓ cup sour cream

1 (14-ounce) can artichoke hearts, drained and finely chopped

1 cup thawed frozen chopped spinach, squeezed of excess liquid

2 cloves garlic, minced

⅔ cup shredded mozzarella

½ cup freshly grated Parmesan

Kosher salt

Pinch crushed red pepper flakes

1 pound refrigerated pizza dough

¼ cup baking soda

1 large egg, mixed with 1 tablespoon water, for brushing

Coarse salt

1. Preheat oven to 400° and grease a large baking sheet with cooking spray.

2. In a large bowl, combine cream cheese, sour cream, artichoke hearts, chopped spinach, garlic, mozzarella, and ¼ cup of Parmesan. Season with salt and red pepper flakes.

3. Divide dough into 4 equal pieces, then divide each piece into 4, making 16 pieces total. Stretch and roll each piece into a long rectangle, then spread about 2 tablespoons spinach-artichoke mixture on top. Pinch and tightly roll, making sure none of mixture is exposed, into a long skinny rope. Twist and shape rope into a pretzel.

4. In a large pot over high heat, combine 4 cups water and baking soda. Bring to a boil, then reduce to a simmer. Add stuffed pretzels and cook 1 minute, stirring gently to prevent sticking. Remove with a slotted spoon and transfer to prepared baking sheet, making sure pretzels aren't touching.

5. Brush egg wash over pretzels and sprinkle with coarse salt and remaining ¼ cup of Parmesan. Bake until deeply golden, 18 to 22 minutes.

CHEESE BALL BITES

DELISH FAVE

TOTAL TIME: 1 HR 15 MIN / MAKES 18

Okay, full disclosure: We were once snobby about cheese balls. We just didn't understand how truly great they could be. Turns out, when studded with bacon and pecans and made mini, they're absolute perfection.

8 slices bacon

1½ (8-ounce) blocks cream cheese, softened

1 cup shredded cheddar cheese

1 teaspoon garlic powder

1 teaspoon paprika

Kosher salt

Freshly ground black pepper

⅓ cup freshly chopped chives

⅓ cup finely chopped pecans

18 pretzel sticks

1. In a large nonstick skillet, cook bacon until crispy, 8 minutes. Drain on a paper towel-lined plate, then finely chop. Set aside.

2. Meanwhile, in a large bowl, stir together cream cheese, cheddar cheese, garlic powder, and paprika and season with salt and pepper. Use a cookie scoop to form mixture into 18 small balls and transfer to a parchment-lined baking sheet. Refrigerate until firm, 1 hour.

3. In a shallow bowl, stir together bacon, chives, and pecans.

4. Roll balls in bacon-chive-pecan mixture, insert a pretzel stick into each, and let come to room temperature 15 minutes before serving. (If not serving right away, loosely cover with plastic wrap and return to fridge.)

CAPRESE GARLIC BREAD

TOTAL TIME: 30 MIN / SERVES 8 TO 10

#SorryNotSorry for making garlic bread even more addictive than it normally is. This is like the winter version of a caprese—baking the tomatoes makes them sweeter, so it doesn't matter if they're in season.

1 loaf ciabatta, halved lengthwise

½ cup (1 stick) butter, softened

2 cloves garlic, minced

1 tablespoon freshly chopped parsley

Kosher salt

Freshly ground black pepper

¼ cup balsamic vinegar

1 tablespoon honey

1½ cups shredded mozzarella

2 large tomatoes, sliced

Extra-virgin olive oil, for drizzling

Thinly sliced fresh basil, for garnish

1. Preheat oven to 350°F and place ciabatta cut-sides up on a large baking sheet.

2. In a medium bowl, stir together butter, garlic, and parsley and season with salt and pepper. Spread on ciabatta halves and bake until golden, 15 to 20 minutes.

3. Meanwhile, in a small saucepan, simmer balsamic vinegar and honey, stirring occasionally, until reduced by half, 8 to 10 minutes (glaze should be thick enough to coat back of a spoon). Let cool.

4. Top toasted ciabatta with mozzarella and tomatoes and bake until cheese is melty, 5 to 10 minutes more.

5. Drizzle garlic bread with oil and balsamic glaze, garnish with basil, and slice.

USE THAT GLAZE! A batch will keep in the fridge for a few weeks—drizzle it over ricotta cheese, grilled peaches, or leftover pizza.

CHAPTER THREE

FUN DIPS

PRETZEL RING BEER CHEESE DIP

TOTAL TIME: 45 MIN / SERVES 8

DELISH FAVE

Not to brag, but we pretty much feel like we invented the ring dip, a skillet dip surrounded by a ring of bread, biscuits, or even pigs in a blanket. It's become our drunk food specialty—and our favorite way to serve dip at a party, by far. These pretzeled biscuits look impressive, but it's the beer cheese inside that no one will stop talking about.

1¾ cups shredded cheddar cheese, divided

½ cup shredded mozzarella

1 (8-ounce) block cream cheese, softened

1½ tablespoons Dijon mustard

2 tablespoons freshly chopped chives, plus more for garnish

2 teaspoons garlic powder

¼ cup pale ale beer (we love Sierra Nevada)

Kosher salt

Freshly ground black pepper

1 (16.3-ounce) can refrigerated biscuits

2 tablespoons baking soda

1 large egg, mixed with 1 tablespoon water, for brushing biscuits

Coarse salt

Freshly chopped chives

1. Preheat oven to 350°F.

2. In a large bowl, stir together 1½ cups of cheddar cheese, mozzarella, cream cheese, Dijon, chives, garlic powder, and beer and season with salt and pepper.

3. Halve each biscuit and roll into a ball, then slice an X across the top.

4. In a small saucepan, bring 2 cups water and baking soda to a boil and whisk to dissolve. Immediately reduce heat to maintain a simmer. Add biscuits in batches and cook until puffy, 1 minute, then remove with a slotted spoon and transfer to a 10- or 12-inch oven-safe skillet, forming a ring along the inside edge.

5. Brush biscuits with egg wash and sprinkle with coarse salt. Transfer dip to center of skillet and sprinkle with remaining ¼ cup cheddar cheese.

6. Bake until biscuits are golden and dip is bubbly, 33 to 35 minutes.

7. Garnish with chives before serving.

CRAB-ARTICHOKE DIP

TOTAL TIME: 35 MIN / SERVES 8

We have a total fascination with the novel that is The Cheesecake Factory's menu—and it's a constant source of inspiration in our test kitchen. This dip is a riff on one of the chain's most beloved appetizers.

1 (8-ounce) block cream cheese, softened

1 cup mayonnaise

1½ cups shredded Monterey jack cheese, divided

½ cup freshly grated Parmesan

1 (14-ounce) can artichoke hearts, drained and finely chopped

2 cloves garlic, minced

12 ounces lump crabmeat

2 green onions, thinly sliced

2 teaspoons Worcestershire sauce

Kosher salt

Freshly ground black pepper

Freshly chopped parsley, for garnish

Garlicky Crostini

1. Preheat oven to 425°F.

2. In a large bowl, stir together cream cheese, mayonnaise, 1 cup of Monterey jack cheese, Parmesan, artichoke hearts, garlic, crabmeat, green onions, and Worcestershire and season with salt and pepper.

3. Transfer mixture to a 10- or 12-inch oven-safe skillet and sprinkle with remaining ½ cup Monterey jack cheese. Bake until golden and bubbly, 15 to 20 minutes.

4. Garnish with parsley and serve with Garlicky Crostini.

GARLICKY CROSTINI

On a large baking sheet, drizzle a sliced **BAGUETTE** with **OLIVE OIL** and season with **SALT**. Bake at 350°F until golden and toasted, 10 minutes. Immediately rub with a whole **GARLIC CLOVE** (the flavor will soak into the bread!).

WTF?

DONUT GRILLED CHEESE

CLINTON HALL / New York, NY

The chefs at Clinton Hall seem to operate under a "You say jump, we say how high" mentality. They manage to elevate any gastropub classic—like a burger with fries—into a social media spectacle. So when it came time to add a grilled cheese-and-tomato soup combo to the menu, the Clinton Hall team jumped REALLY high. Chefs actually slice a glazed donut in half, pile shredded mozzarella on top, and heat it on a griddle until you can't tell where the sugar stops and the cheese begins. The whole thing is then placed on a banana holder—the sandwich's hole hooks right onto the peg—that hangs over a mini saucepan. And when gravity takes over, the still-steaming cheese oozes out from between the donut halves and into the hot soup below.

GREEK FETA DIP

TOTAL TIME: 20 MIN / SERVES 8

When Lindsay, our deputy editor, served this dip at a girls' night, her friends freaked out—and then three of them emailed her the next day for the recipe (our true marker of success). If you've ever tasted whipped feta, you'll know why.

12 ounces feta cheese

1 cup Greek yogurt

1 (8-ounce) block cream cheese, softened

¼ cup extra-virgin olive oil, plus more for drizzling

Juice and zest of 1 lemon

Kosher salt

Pinch crushed red pepper flakes

2 tablespoons freshly chopped dill, plus more for garnish

½ cup chopped cucumber

½ cup cherry tomatoes, halved

Pita chips, for serving

1. In a large bowl using a hand mixer, beat feta cheese, Greek yogurt, cream cheese, oil, and lemon juice and zest until fluffy and combined. Season with salt and red pepper flakes and stir in dill.

2. Transfer dip to a serving bowl and top with cucumber, tomatoes, dill, and a drizzle of oil.

3. Serve with pita chips.

You don't *have* to bust out your **HAND MIXER** for this, but true whipped feta needs a machine's touch. If you're too lazy, it's totally fine to use a spoon.

TRIPLE-CHEESE BACON SPINACH DIP

TOTAL TIME: 45 MIN / SERVES 8

DELISH FAVE

This is one of our most popular dips of all time. It's probably because it has more bacon and cheese than any spinach dip ever should—LOL, said no one ever.

10 slices bacon

1 (8-ounce) block cream cheese, softened

⅓ cup mayonnaise

⅓ cup sour cream

1 teaspoon garlic powder

1 teaspoon paprika

Kosher salt

Freshly ground black pepper

1 pound frozen chopped spinach, thawed and squeezed of excess liquid

1 cup freshly grated Parmesan

1 cup shredded mozzarella, divided

1. Preheat oven to 350°F.

2. In a large nonstick skillet over medium heat, cook bacon until crispy, 8 minutes. Drain on a paper towel-lined plate, then chop.

3. In a large bowl, stir together cream cheese, mayonnaise, sour cream, garlic powder, and paprika and season with salt and pepper. Fold in chopped spinach, bacon, Parmesan, and ¾ cup of mozzarella.

4. Transfer dip to a baking dish and sprinkle with remaining ¼ cup mozzarella. Bake until golden and bubbly, 25 to 30 minutes.

5. Serve with crostini (see page 71).

WANT *MORE* CHEESE? This dip also works so well with white cheddar, fontina, or provolone.

HOT REUBEN DIP

TOTAL TIME: 30 MIN / SERVES 8

Reuben is one of those flavor profiles that generally gets ignored (why should Buffalo or cheesesteak have all the fun?). But we love the mix of salty corned beef, bitter sauerkraut, and melty Swiss. The combo is perfect for a dip.

1 (8-ounce) block cream cheese, softened

½ cup Russian (or Thousand Island) dressing

1¼ cups shredded Swiss cheese, divided

1 cup chopped corned beef, divided

1 cup sauerkraut, drained

Freshly ground black pepper

Freshly chopped parsley, for garnish

Bagel chips, for serving

1. Preheat oven to 350°F.

2. In a medium bowl, stir together cream cheese and Russian dressing until combined, then fold in 1 cup of Swiss, almost all the corned beef, and sauerkraut and season with pepper.

3. Transfer dip to a small baking dish and top with remaining ¼ cup Swiss and corned beef. Bake until golden and bubbly, 18 to 20 minutes.

4. Garnish with parsley and serve with bagel chips.

EGGPLANT PARM DIP

TOTAL TIME: 1 HR 20 MIN / SERVES 8

This isn't the prettiest dip ever, but damn, is it delish. Don't stress about having to roast the garlic—do it while you're cooking the eggplant, and use the 40 minutes to sneak in an episode of *Stranger Things*.

1 head garlic, top sliced off to expose cloves

Extra-virgin olive oil, for drizzling

2 large eggplants

1 cup marinara

2½ cups shredded mozzarella, divided

½ cup freshly grated Parmesan, divided

¼ cup packed fresh basil leaves, plus sliced basil for garnish

Kosher salt

Freshly ground black pepper

¼ cup panko breadcrumbs

Sliced baguette, for serving

1. Preheat oven to 400°F and line a large baking sheet with foil.

2. Drizzle garlic with oil, wrap in foil to completely enclose, and set on the prepared baking sheet. Put eggplants on baking sheet with garlic.

3. Bake until eggplants are soft and blistered and garlic is caramelized, about 40 minutes. Let cool slightly.

4. Split open eggplants and scoop out flesh into a food processor or blender; discard skins. Squeeze out garlic cloves and add to food processor (or blender) along with marinara, 1 cup of shredded mozzarella, ¼ cup of Parmesan, and the whole basil leaves and season generously with salt and pepper. Process until smooth, then transfer mixture to a baking dish and sprinkle with remaining 1½ cups mozzarella, ¼ cup Parm, and breadcrumbs. Drizzle with oil.

5. Bake until golden and bubbly, 25 minutes.

6. Garnish with sliced basil and serve with baguette.

BLT
GUACAMOLE

5 WAYS TO MAKE GUACAMOLE

Classic guac never gets old—but these ideas are next-level.

1
BLT

In a large bowl, mash 4 avocados until almost smooth. Stir in ½ cup halved cherry tomatoes, ½ cup shredded romaine lettuce, 4 slices cooked and chopped bacon, 2 sliced green onions, and juice of 1 lime and season with salt and pepper.

2
CAPRESE

In a large bowl, mash 4 avocados until almost smooth. Stir in ½ cup chopped mini mozzarella balls, ½ cup halved cherry tomatoes, juice of 1 lime, and 1 clove minced garlic, and season with salt. Top with freshly torn basil.

3
BUFFALO

In a large bowl, mash 4 avocados until almost smooth. Stir in ¼ cup crumbled blue cheese, juice of 1 lime, 1 clove minced garlic, and 1 tablespoon Buffalo sauce and season with salt.

4
GREEK

In a large bowl, mash 4 avocados until almost smooth. Stir in ½ cup chopped cucumber, ½ cup chopped tomatoes, ¼ cup crumbled feta cheese, ¼ cup chopped kalamata olives, juice of 1 lemon, 2 tablespoons freshly chopped parsley, 1 tablespoon freshly chopped dill, and 2 teaspoons dried oregano and season with salt and pepper.

5
HAWAIIAN

In a large bowl, mash 4 avocados until almost smooth. Stir in ¾ cup chopped pineapple, ¾ cup chopped mangoes, ¼ cup diced red onion, ¼ cup freshly chopped cilantro, juice of 1 lime, and 1 minced jalapeño and season with salt.

GARLICKY SHRIMP DIP

TOTAL TIME: 40 MIN / SERVES 8

Some would consider this a poor man's crab dip, but there's nothing cheap about it: The lemony-garlic shrimp and melty mozz will make you feel like a million bucks.

- 2 tablespoons extra-virgin olive oil
- 1 pound medium shrimp, thawed if frozen, peeled and deveined
- 3 cloves garlic, minced
- Kosher salt
- Freshly ground black pepper
- 1 (8-ounce) block cream cheese, softened
- ¼ cup mayonnaise
- ¾ cup shredded mozzarella
- ¼ cup freshly grated Parmesan
- Juice and zest of 1 lemon
- 2 tablespoons freshly chopped parsley, plus more for garnish
- Pita chips, for serving

1. Preheat oven to 350°F.

2. In a large skillet over medium heat, heat oil. Add shrimp and garlic and season with salt and pepper. Cook until shrimp is pink and no longer opaque, 3 to 4 minutes. Let cool slightly, then coarsely chop.

3. In a large bowl, stir together cream cheese, mayonnaise, mozzarella, Parmesan, lemon juice and zest, parsley, and chopped shrimp and season with salt and pepper.

4. Transfer dip to a small baking dish and bake until golden and bubbly, 25 minutes.

5. Garnish with parsley and serve with pita chips.

> I'll never forget the time I blacked out and ate all the shrimp dip. Or the time I blacked out and ate an entire Texas sheet cake. Clearly there's been a lot of blacking out and eating entire skillets. No regrets. —JULIA

PIZZA DIP

TOTAL TIME: 45 MIN / SERVES 8

When trying to figure out what dessert to make Lindsay for her birthday, nothing sweet felt as right as this dip—so we skipped a cake altogether and just stuck a bunch of candles straight in here. It's everything you love about sliced pepperoni pizza baked with ricotta and Parm.

2 cups shredded mozzarella, divided

1 (8-ounce) block cream cheese, softened

½ cup ricotta

¼ cup plus 1 tablespoon freshly grated Parmesan, divided

1 tablespoon Italian seasoning

½ teaspoon crushed red pepper flakes

Kosher salt

¼ cup pizza sauce or marinara

¼ cup sliced pepperoni

Sliced baguette, for serving

1. Preheat oven to 350°F.

2. In a large bowl, stir together 1¼ cups of mozzarella, cream cheese, ricotta, ¼ cup of Parmesan, Italian seasoning, and red pepper flakes and season with salt.

3. Transfer dip to a small oven-safe skillet or baking dish and spoon over pizza sauce. Top with remaining ¾ cup mozzarella and 1 tablespoon Parmesan, and pepperoni.

4. Bake until golden and bubbly, 25 to 30 minutes.

5. Let cool 10 minutes, then blot any grease from pepperoni (or don't!) before serving with baguette.

TOP THIS DIP with literally anything you like: black beans, pimientos, sour cream, cotija . . .

TEXAS TRASH DIP

TOTAL TIME: 40 MIN / SERVES 8

You'd be surprised by how often we start with a crazy recipe name and work backward to figure out what would be in it. "Trash" doesn't generally evoke "delicious," but don't be fooled: This Southwestern dip is a real winner.

1 (8-ounce) block cream cheese, softened

1 cup sour cream

2 (16-ounce) cans refried beans, drained

1 (7-ounce) can chopped green chiles, drained

½ cup corn (drained, if using canned)

1 teaspoon ground cumin

1 teaspoon chili powder

1 teaspoon dried oregano

½ teaspoon paprika

Kosher salt

Freshly ground black pepper

2 cups shredded Monterey jack cheese, divided

2 cups shredded cheddar cheese, divided

TOPPINGS
Sliced black olives

Halved cherry tomatoes

Diced avocado

Thinly sliced green onions

1. Preheat oven to 350°F.

2. In a large bowl, stir together cream cheese, sour cream, beans, chiles, corn, and spices and season with salt and pepper. Fold in 1 cup each of both cheeses.

3. Transfer dip to a small baking dish and top with remaining 1 cup each of both cheeses. Bake until golden and bubbly, 25 to 30 minutes.

4. Garnish with desired toppings before serving.

> **"You dip the way you want to dip, I'll dip the way I want to dip."**
> **—GEORGE COSTANZA, *SEINFELD***

SUPER BREAD BOWL DIP

TOTAL TIME: 55 MIN / SERVES 12

When we came up with this for Super Bowl 50, we legitimately thought the idea was going to break the Internet. And to be honest, it kind of did: Our audience lost their minds, and word on the street was that the French bread dough we used was flying off supermarket shelves.

FOR THE BREAD BOWL

3 (11-ounce) tubes refrigerated French bread dough

1 large egg, mixed with 1 tablespoon water, for brushing dough

FOR THE DIP

1 bunch kale, leaves stripped from stems and chopped (about 6 cups)

1 (15-ounce) can artichoke hearts, drained and chopped

1 (8-ounce) block cream cheese, softened

1½ cups shredded white cheddar cheese

½ cup freshly grated Parmesan

½ cup ricotta

2 cloves garlic, minced

Kosher salt

Freshly ground black pepper

Pita chips, for serving

1. Preheat oven to 350°F.

2. Make bread bowl: Roll out 1 tube dough into a sheet. Form a football shape on top with remaining tubes dough and toothpick the sides. Trim excess and use to form laces. Brush dough all over with egg wash.

3. Bake until bread is lightly golden, about 20 minutes.

4. Meanwhile, make dip: In a large pot of boiling water, blanch kale leaves, 1 minute. Drain and pat dry with paper towels.

5. In a large bowl, stir together blanched kale, artichoke hearts, cream cheese, cheddar cheese, Parmesan, ricotta, and garlic and season with salt and pepper.

6. Transfer dip to baked bread bowl, top with laces, and bake until golden and bubbly, 15 to 20 minutes.

7. Serve with pita chips.

CHAPTER FOUR

'WICHES, BITCHES

CHICKEN PARM BURGERS

TOTAL TIME: 30 MIN / SERVES 4

These are for everyone who loves the idea of making chicken Parm but who don't actually want to deal with the whole dredging thing. The chicken patties simmer in marinara, so they'll never turn out dry.

1 pound ground chicken

½ cup Italian breadcrumbs

¼ cup freshly chopped parsley

2 cloves garlic, minced

¼ cup freshly grated Parmesan

Kosher salt

Freshly ground black pepper

1 tablespoon vegetable oil

2 cups marinara, plus more for buns

¾ cup shredded mozzarella

4 hamburger buns, toasted

Freshly sliced basil, for garnish

1. In a medium bowl, stir together chicken, breadcrumbs, garlic, parsley, and Parmesan and season with salt and pepper. Form into 4 patties.

2. In a large skillet over medium-high heat, heat oil. Cook patties until bottoms are golden, 4 to 5 minutes, then flip and add marinara to skillet. Bring to a simmer (reduce heat to medium if sauce is bubbling too rapidly) and top each patty evenly with mozzarella. Cover and cook until chicken is cooked through and cheese melts, 10 to 12 minutes more.

3. Spoon sauce from skillet onto bottom halves of burger buns and place patties on top. Top with basil and burger bun tops.

GREEK GRILLED CHEESE

TOTAL TIME: 25 MIN / SERVES 4

The grilled cheese that can trick you into thinking you're eating halfway healthy. Hey, Greek purists: Yes, we know Greek dishes don't have mozzarella, but we're turning a blind eye on this one.

Softened butter, for bread

8 slices sourdough bread

3 cups shredded mozzarella

1 cup crumbled feta cheese

1 (16-ounce) jar roasted red peppers, drained and chopped

½ cup pitted kalamata olives, halved

2 tablespoons freshly torn dill

1. Butter one side of each bread slice. In a large skillet over medium heat, add one slice bread, butter-side down. Top with a quarter each of the mozzarella, feta cheese, roasted red peppers, kalamata olives, and dill. Top with another bread slice, butter-side up, and cook until bread is golden and cheese is melty, 2 to 3 minutes. Flip and cook until golden, 2 to 3 minutes more.

2. Repeat with remaining ingredients to make 4 sandwiches total.

"I'm into grilled cheese. Grilled cheese makes me feel beautiful."

—EMMA STONE

BACON WEAVE BLT

TOTAL TIME: 50 MIN / SERVES 4

This is going to sound nuts, but we find the process of weaving bacon oddly therapeutic. But we're not asking you to weave it for your sanity: We insist you do it because it means bacon in every. single. bite.

12 slices thin bacon, cut in half

2 tablespoons maple syrup

8 slices sourdough bread, toasted

2 tablespoons mayonnaise

4 large lettuce leaves

2 medium tomatoes, sliced

Kosher salt

Freshly ground black pepper

> I can't tell you how many times I've gotten on the train after work and thought to myself incredulously: "Why does this train smell like bacon?" It's me. It's ALWAYS me.
> **—LENA**

1. Preheat oven to 400°F. Line a baking sheet with foil and place a wire rack on top.

2. To form one bacon weave, line up 3 bacon halves side by side on prepared pan. Lift up one end of middle bacon slice and place a fourth bacon half underneath that slice and on top of the other two pieces. Place middle slice back down, then lift up the ends of two other strips and place a fifth bacon half on top of the middle piece and underneath the sides Ⓐ. Lay slices back down Ⓑ. Finally, lift other end of the middle slice and place a sixth bacon half on top of the side pieces and underneath the middle slice Ⓒ. Repeat with remaining bacon to make 3 more weaves Ⓓ.

3. Bake 30 minutes, then remove pan from oven and brush bacon with maple syrup. Continue baking until bacon is beginning to crisp and cook through, about 10 minutes more.

4. Spread mayonnaise on one side of each bread slice. Top 4 slices with lettuce and tomatoes and season with salt and pepper. Top with bacon weave and a second bread slice, mayo-side down.

WATCH & LEARN

Ⓐ Ⓑ Ⓒ Ⓓ

We love thick-cut bacon, but bacon weaves work best with the **THIN STUFF.**

BACON-STUFFED BURGERS

TOTAL TIME: 45 MIN / SERVES 4

We've always thought of Guy Fieri as our cooking soul mate—he's not afraid to mix up some madness—and he has a bacon-chorizo-stuffed burger that's as over-the-top as he is. The only problem: It's kind of time-consuming. So we channeled him when we developed this simpler version: You just sauté bacon, onion, and garlic and start stuffing.

8 slices bacon

1 medium onion, chopped

2 cloves garlic, minced

4 slices cheddar cheese, quartered

1½ pounds ground beef

Kosher salt

Freshly ground black pepper

1 tablespoon vegetable oil

4 sesame buns, split

Sliced tomatoes, for serving

Lettuce, for serving

Pickles, for serving

1. In a large nonstick skillet over medium heat, cook bacon until crispy, 8 minutes. Drain on a paper towel–lined plate, then chop. Pour off about half the bacon fat from the pan, add onion, and cook, stirring, until soft, about 5 minutes. Stir in garlic and cook until fragrant, 1 minute more. Remove from heat and stir in bacon.

2. Divide beef into 8 equal portions and flatten each into a large, thin patty. Top one patty with 2 pieces cheddar cheese, a heaping spoonful of bacon mixture, and another 2 pieces cheddar cheese. Place a second patty on top and pinch edges to seal. Repeat with remaining patties and cheese to make 8 burgers total.

3. Season both sides of burgers generously with salt and pepper. Refrigerate until ready to cook.

4. In a large skillet over medium-high heat, heat oil. Add burgers and cook until seared and crusty on bottom, about 5 minutes. Flip, reduce heat to medium, cover, and cook until burgers are cooked to your liking, about 6 minutes more for medium.

5. Serve each burger on a bun with tomatoes, lettuce, and pickles.

③① WAYS TO TOP A BURGER

WE ALL LOOK BACK WITH HORROR on the day Jo and Lindsay cooked and topped a hundred burgers in the test kitchen. (By the end, they reeked of smoke and seemed to be suffering from a mild form of carbon monoxide poisoning.) But we all learned an important lesson: You can put practically anything on a burger and it'll taste amazing. These are our favorites.

GRUYÈRE + CARAMELIZED ONIONS + MUSHROOMS

1
GRUYÈRE +
CARAMELIZED
ONIONS +
MUSHROOMS

2
MARINARA
+ SLICED
PEPPERONI

3
SAUTÉED
SPINACH +
STEAK SAUCE

4
CRISPY FRIED
ONIONS

5
FETA CHEESE
+ KALAMATA
OLIVES

6
FRIED EGG +
SRIRACHA

7
BACON +
MAPLE SYRUP

8
MANGO +
AVOCADO

9
MELTED
PEANUT
BUTTER

10
COLESLAW
+ BARBECUE
SAUCE

11
TERIYAKI
SAUCE +
SESAME SEEDS

12
BUFFALO
SAUCE +
BLUE CHEESE

13
PEANUT SAUCE
+ GREEN
ONIONS

14
BRIE +
APRICOT JAM

15
MAC 'N'
CHEESE

16
SAUERKRAUT
+ RUSSIAN
DRESSING

17
QUESO +
PICKLED
JALAPEÑOS

18
CANNED
CHILI

19
CREAM CHEESE
+ EVERYTHING
BAGEL
SEASONING

20
PICO DE GALLO
+ TORTILLA
CHIPS

21
TATER TOTS
+ CHEDDAR
CHEESE

22
PEANUT
BUTTER +
BACON

23
NUTELLA

24
HONEY
MUSTARD +
SLICED APPLES

25
PESTO +
MOZZARELLA

26
CHIMICHURRI
SAUCE

27
PULLED PORK
+ PICKLES

28
CAESAR
DRESSING +
ANCHOVIES

> "Hamburgers!
> The cornerstone
> of any nutritious
> breakfast!"
>
> —JULES WINNFIELD,
> *PULP FICTION*

29
GUACAMOLE +
PEPPER JACK
CHEESE

30
HAM +
PINEAPPLE

31
RANCH +
WAFFLE FRIES

CRAB CAKE BURGERS

TOTAL TIME: 25 MIN / SERVES 4

Crab cakes might seem kinda old school, but when transformed into a burger, they're cool again. We like to keep it simple with lettuce and our Old Bay Sauce—but feel free to go crazy with bacon or pickled jalapeños.

1 pound lump crabmeat

⅓ cup breadcrumbs

⅓ cup mayonnaise

1 large egg, lightly beaten

¼ cup finely chopped chives

1 tablespoon Worcestershire sauce

Kosher salt

Freshly ground black pepper

2 tablespoons extra-virgin olive oil

4 burger buns, split

4 pieces Bibb lettuce

Old Bay Sauce

1. In a large bowl, stir together crabmeat, breadcrumbs, mayonnaise, egg, chives, and Worcestershire and season with salt and pepper. Form into 4 patties.

2. In a large skillet over medium-high heat, heat oil. Cook burgers until golden, about 5 minutes per side.

3. Serve burgers on buns with lettuce and Old Bay Sauce.

I DON'T LIKE TO SHARE— I'M PRETTY SHELLFISH.

OLD BAY SAUCE

In a small bowl, combine 3 tablespoons **MAYONNAISE**, juice of ½ **LEMON**, 1 tablespoon **DILL PICKLE RELISH**, and 1 tablespoon **OLD BAY SEASONING**.

GIANT PARTY SUB

TOTAL TIME: 35 MIN / SERVES 10

Jo asked us to try this bread technique (bake French bread dough in a Bundt pan for one HUGE sandwich bun), and everyone thought it was nuts. But you listen to the boss—and when it turned out amazing, Jo got to say, "I told you so," and Delish gave birth to one of its bizarre specialties: giant sandwiches. We've used this technique for grilled cheese, Philly cheesesteak, and even a massive bacon-egg-and-cheese.

Cooking spray

2 (11-ounce) tubes refrigerated French bread dough

3 tablespoons extra-virgin olive oil, divided

2 tablespoons red wine vinegar, divided

1 teaspoon Italian seasoning, divided

¼ pound sliced provolone cheese

½ pound sliced salami

½ pound deli-sliced ham

½ pound thinly sliced pepperoni

1½ cups shredded romaine lettuce

2 large beefsteak tomatoes, sliced

1 teaspoon toasted sesame seeds

1. Preheat oven to 350°F and grease a Bundt pan with cooking spray.

2. Place bread dough into bottom of prepared pan and pinch together ends to form a ring.

3. Bake until golden brown and cooked through, 25 to 30 minutes. Let cool 5 minutes, then invert onto a wire rack to cool completely.

4. Place baked bread on a serving platter and slice in half to make two layers. Drizzle bottom half with 1 tablespoon each of oil and vinegar and sprinkle with ¼ teaspoon of Italian seasoning. Top with provolone cheese, salami, ham, pepperoni, lettuce, and tomatoes. Drizzle with another 1 tablespoon each of oil and vinegar and sprinkle with remaining ¾ teaspoon Italian seasoning.

5. Sandwich with top half of baked bread and brush with remaining 1 tablespoon oil. Sprinkle with sesame seeds and slice.

INSIDE THE DELISH KITCHEN

Peek behind the doors of most test kitchens and you probably won't find an Oreo drawer. But when you're in the Delish Test Kitchen, to get to the spices, you have to get through **15 kinds of sprinkles** first. This 100-square-foot space is crammed corner-to-corner with both the everyday and the bizarre. The ingredients we use consistently: **12 jars of pickles**, **20 bags of chocolate chips**, and **40 blocks of cream cheese**. The random: A **giant tub of Twizzlers**, a **donkey piñata**, and a **framed mantra** that you should "eat like no one will ever see you naked." Consider yourself warned: When you're in our house, you better eat like a local and follow the rules.

PIGS IN A QUILT

TOTAL TIME: 45 MIN / SERVES 8

You guys, it's a HOT DOG WEAVE! If you're looking for an inventive way to serve dogs at a party, this is it.

Cooking spray

All-purpose flour, for dusting

1 (11-ounce) tube refrigerated French bread dough

12 hot dogs

1 tablespoon melted butter

Coarse salt, for sprinkling

Yellow mustard, for serving

1. Preheat oven to 375°F and line a baking sheet with parchment paper. Grease parchment with cooking spray.

2. On a lightly floured surface, unroll bread dough, then cut in half crosswise. Cut each half crosswise into 8 thin strips Ⓐ. Transfer first set of strips to prepared baking sheet.

3. Fold back every other strip and lay down a hot dog Ⓑ. Bring strips back over hot dog and fold back alternate strips Ⓒ. Lay down second hot dog and repeat weave process until you've reached the end of the strips with 6 hot dogs Ⓓ. Repeat to make second quilt.

4. Trim sides of dough, brush dough with melted butter, and sprinkle with coarse salt. Bake until deeply golden, 16 to 18 minutes.

5. Cut into squares and serve with mustard.

WATCH & LEARN

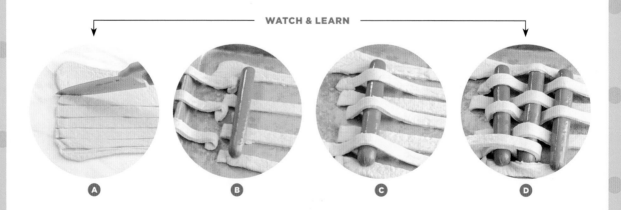

Ⓐ Ⓑ Ⓒ Ⓓ

MOZZ-STUFFED MEATBALL SUBS

TOTAL TIME: 45 MIN / SERVES 4

When you want to Netflix, chill, and be cozy AF, these hoagies are everything.

1 pound ground beef

1 cup breadcrumbs

¼ cup freshly grated Parmesan, plus more for serving

2 tablespoons freshly chopped parsley, plus more for serving

2 cloves garlic, minced

1 large egg

Kosher salt

Freshly ground black pepper

4 ounces mozzarella or 4 mozzarella sticks, cut into small cubes

1 tablespoon extra-virgin olive oil

½ cup marinara

4 hoagie rolls

1. Preheat oven to 450°F.

2. In a large bowl, combine ground beef, breadcrumbs, Parmesan, parsley, garlic, and egg and season with salt and pepper. Mix until just combined, then form into meatballs.

3. Press 1 cube mozzarella into center of a meatball, sealing meat tightly around cheese. Transfer to a large baking sheet and repeat with remaining mozz and meatballs.

4. Drizzle meatballs with oil and bake until cooked through, about 15 minutes.

5. Spoon marinara onto each roll. Bake until bread is toasty, 2 to 3 minutes. Top each hoagie roll with 4 or 5 meatballs, then sprinkle with Parmesan and parsley.

WTF?

MOZZARELLA STICK BUN BURGER

BUNS BAR / New York, NY

When your restaurant is called Buns Bar, you'd better bring it in the burger department. This tiny Manhattan joint serves up eighteen different sliders and burgers sandwiched between just about every type of bun: grilled sourdough bread, pretzel, steamed bao buns—even a donut. But co-owner Luke Pascal got inspired by the fried mozzarella triangles served at Buns Bar's sister restaurant, Chuck and Blade. "I just turned to our chef one day and said, 'We should put a burger on that,'" he says. And that's how the 21st Century Burger came to be: a 10-ounce beef patty with lettuce and tomato that's served between two deep-fried slabs of cheese, which are essentially giant mozzarella sticks. "It was my way of reinventing the cheeseburger," Pascal says. The only thing better than eating this epic mash-up of bar foods is the epic cheese-pull shot you get for Instagram.

GRILLED CHEESE DOGS

TOTAL TIME: 20 MIN / SERVES 4

File away this brilliant mash-up as a must-try
on your next cheat day. (So, tomorrow?)

---

4 hot dog buns

2 tablespoons butter, softened

¼ teaspoon garlic powder

¼ teaspoon onion powder

4 hot dogs, split lengthwise (be careful to not cut all the way through)

3 cups shredded cheddar cheese

4 green onions, sliced

1. Flatten hot dog buns with a rolling pin. In a small bowl, stir together butter, garlic powder, and onion powder. Spread all over outsides of buns.

2. In a large skillet over medium heat, sear hot dogs (working in batches if necessary) until charred, 2 minutes per side. Set aside.

3. Place a bun buttered-side down in skillet and top with ½ cup of cheddar cheese, a hot dog, a little more cheddar cheese, and ¼ of green onions.

4. Cover and cook over medium heat until cheese melts, then use a spatula to close the bun. Repeat with remaining ingredients to make 4 cheese dogs total.

THIS ONE'S A REAL WEINER!

MAKE THEM FANCIER with Gruyère and caramelized onions or provolone cheese and peppers.

INSIDE THE
SONIC
SKATE-OFF

Every time Josh Tucker laces up, he thinks of his grandfather. "He was a really big disco skater, and I wanted to be just like him," the Dothan, Alabama, native remembers. But rather than sequined bell bottoms, Tucker (top right) dons a red-and-blue uniform and spins a tray full of fast food. Tucker is a Sonic Carhop—a skater waiter.

Sonic is known as much for its Coneys and chili cheese fries as it is for the people who deliver them. The waiters-on-wheels shtick has been around for decades, and for Tucker, it's home. "I feel like me when I'm on my skates there," he says. He's been skating since he was three. But after Tucker joined Sonic's team, it went from hobby to competitive sport.

The chain hosts an annual competition for its most talented Carhops to show off their chops, navigating a twelve-part obstacle course while balancing a full meal. They're judged on technical skill and flair, and 2017 was Tucker's year. The one before, he'd narrowly missed winning the title. "This year, I studied film like I was going to play football at Alabama," Tucker laughs. One of the four other competitors was a fellow Dothan Carhop, Lydell "Rocket" Dyess, who had moved to the small Alabama city to learn new moves from Tucker.

It paid off: Dyess took home the silver, but it was Tucker who finally got gold. He has no plans to compete again—but he's still got a mission to fulfill: "I want people to understand: Roller skating is not dead."

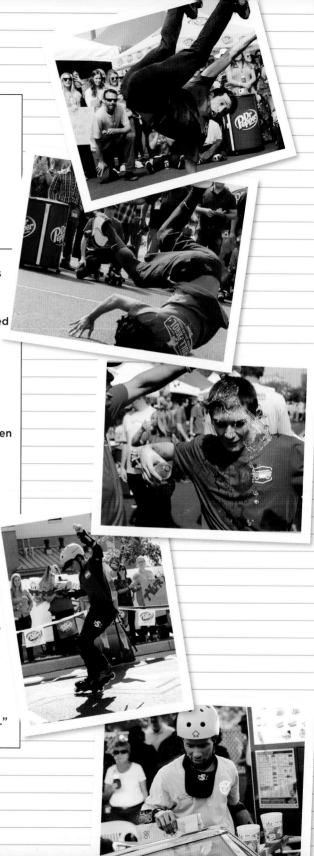

CHICKEN CHEESESTEAKS

TOTAL TIME: 25 MIN / SERVES 4

When we posted this video, Philadelphia folks DESTROYED us for swapping out steak for chicken here ("These aren't real cheesesteaks!!"). Then Philly-born trio Boyz II Men came to visit our test kitchen, and they told us that chicken cheesesteaks are their favorite. (Insert gloating face here.)

1 tablespoon extra-virgin olive oil

1 large onion, chopped

3 bell peppers (red and green), chopped

Kosher salt

Freshly ground black pepper

1 pound boneless, skinless chicken breasts, thinly sliced

1 tablespoon Italian seasoning

6 or 7 slices provolone cheese

4 hoagie rolls

1. In a large skillet over medium heat, heat oil. Add onion and peppers and season with salt and pepper. Cook, stirring occasionally, until very soft, 8 to 10 minutes.

2. Add chicken and Italian seasoning and stir to combine. Cook, stirring occasionally, until chicken is golden and no longer pink inside, about 10 minutes.

3. Cover chicken and peppers with provolone cheese and cover to let melt, 1 minute.

4. Serve on hoagie rolls.

EGG-IN-A-HOLE BURGERS

TOTAL TIME: 30 MIN / SERVES 4

Breakfast burgers have been done a million times before, but nothing compares to this hack: You hollow out a burger patty, crack an egg right inside, and say good-bye to your hangover.

---

1 pound ground beef

Kosher salt

Freshly ground black pepper

2 tablespoons butter

4 large eggs

4 slices cheddar cheese

3 tablespoons mayonnaise

1 tablespoon Sriracha

4 hamburger buns, split and toasted

8 slices bacon, cooked

4 leaves lettuce

1. Form beef into 3 equal-size patties. Using a small glass, cut out center of each patty to create a donut shape; combine excess meat to form a fourth patty and cut out center. Season patties generously with salt and pepper.

2. In a large skillet over medium-high heat, melt butter. Add patties and cook 2 minutes, then flip. Crack an egg into center of each, season with salt and pepper, cover, and cook until egg whites are set, about 5 minutes more. Top with cheddar cheese and cover with lid to let melt, 1 minute.

3. In a small bowl, stir together mayonnaise and Sriracha. Spread on toasted buns.

4. Serve burgers on toasted buns with cooked bacon and lettuce.

Leave a little bit of the **EGG WHITE** when you add the raw egg to the center of the burger patty. Everything will cook more evenly.

SLOPPY JOE GRILLED CHEESE

TOTAL TIME: 30 MIN / SERVES 4

Any time we make this sandwich at the office (which is too often), Delish staffers act like they've literally never seen food before. If nostalgia could be a sandwich, it'd be this. Best served with potato chips and a cold beer.

1 tablespoon extra-virgin olive oil

1 medium onion, chopped

1 pound ground beef

½ cup ketchup

2 cloves garlic, minced

⅓ cup packed brown sugar

2 tablespoons yellow mustard

1 tablespoon chili powder

Kosher salt

Freshly ground black pepper

Butter, for bread

8 slices sandwich bread

2 cups shredded cheddar cheese

1. In a large skillet over medium heat, heat oil. Add onion and cook, stirring, until soft, about 5 minutes. Add ground beef and cook, stirring and breaking up meat, until no longer pink, 6 to 8 minutes. Drain fat.

2. Return beef mixture to skillet over medium heat and stir in ketchup, garlic, brown sugar, mustard, and chili powder and season with salt and pepper. Simmer until thick, 5 minutes. Transfer mixture to a plate and wipe skillet clean.

3. Assemble sandwiches: Butter one side of each bread slice. Place 1 slice butter-side down in skillet and spoon over sloppy joe mixture. Top with ½ cup of cheddar cheese and one more slice bread, buttered-side up.

4. Cook over medium heat until bread is golden and cheese is melty, about 3 minutes per side. Repeat with remaining ingredients to make 4 sandwiches total.

CHAPTER FIVE

WHAT THE FORK'S FOR DINNER?

You'll literally never ask that question again.

BBQ LIME CHICKEN

TOTAL TIME: 40 MIN / SERVES 6

This sauce—a barbecue sauce that's jacked up with brown sugar,
lime juice, and garlic—holds a special place in our hearts:
It's one of our very first recipes.

1 cup all-purpose flour

2 pounds chicken tenders

2 cups panko breadcrumbs

3 large eggs

Kosher salt

Freshly ground black pepper

1 cup barbecue sauce

½ cup packed brown sugar

Juice of 2 limes

1 teaspoon garlic powder

**Ranch dressing, for serving
(optional)**

1. Preheat oven to 425°F.

2. In a large resealable plastic bag, combine flour and chicken tenders and shake until fully coated.

3. Set up a dredging station: In one shallow bowl, put breadcrumbs, and in another shallow bowl, whisk together eggs and 2 tablespoons water. Dip chicken in egg mixture, then coat in breadcrumbs. Transfer to prepared baking sheet and season generously with salt and pepper.

4. Bake until golden and crispy, 20 to 25 minutes.

5. Meanwhile, in a small saucepan over low heat, whisk together barbecue sauce, brown sugar, lime juice, and garlic powder. Simmer 5 minutes.

6. In a large bowl, toss baked chicken in sauce until coated. Serve with ranch, if desired.

GET SAUCY! This sauce makes everything it touches infinitely more addictive. Try it on Brussels sprouts, pork chops, and burgers.

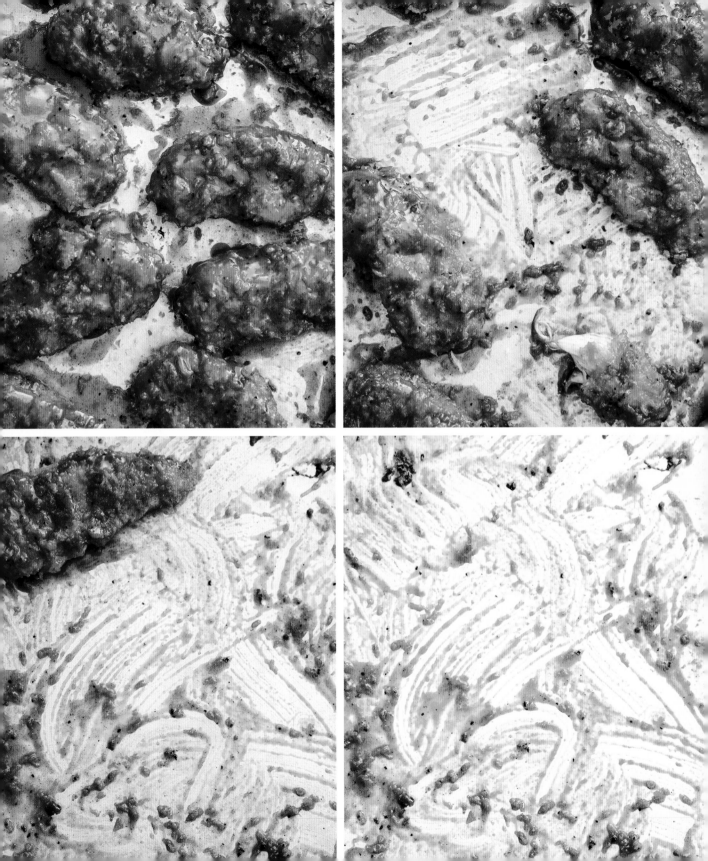

CHICKEN FRIED STEAK FINGERS

TOTAL TIME: 40 MIN / SERVES 4

Jo's husband, Scott, is a huge chicken fried steak fan (Cracker Barrel's is the best, FYI)—so when she stumbled on a version of this recipe, she knew Delish needed to have its own take. The steak strips and gravy dipping sauce make it less of a gut bomb and more of a fun finger food.

1 cup all-purpose flour

1 teaspoon garlic powder

1 teaspoon onion powder

¼ teaspoon paprika

½ teaspoon cayenne pepper

Kosher salt

Freshly ground black pepper

¾ cup milk (preferably whole or 2%)

2 large eggs

1½ pounds cube steak, sliced into ½-inch-thick strips

Vegetable oil, for frying

FOR THE GRAVY

4 tablespoons butter

1¼ cups milk (preferably whole or 2%)

1 tablespoon freshly chopped chives

Kosher salt

Freshly ground black pepper

1. In a shallow bowl, whisk together flour and spices and season with salt and pepper. (Set aside 3 tablespoons for gravy.) In another shallow bowl, whisk together milk and eggs. Season steak generously with salt and pepper. Working in batches, dredge steak thoroughly in flour mixture to coat, then dip in egg mixture. Return steak to flour mixture and dredge once more.

2. In a large deep-sided skillet over medium heat, heat ½ inch oil until shimmering (about 350°F). Using tongs, add steak strips, one by one, and cook, in batches, until completely golden, about 2 minutes per side. Drain on a paper towel–lined plate.

3. Make gravy: In a small skillet over medium heat, melt butter. Whisk in reserved flour mixture and cook until golden, 1 minute. Gradually whisk in milk and bring mixture to a boil. Reduce heat to low and simmer until gravy is thick. Stir in chives and season with salt and pepper.

4. Serve steak "fingers" with gravy for dipping.

MARRY ME CHICKEN

After the camera stopped rolling, Chelsea dug into a skillet of this chicken, turned to Lindsay, and said, "I'd marry you for this chicken." The name stuck because it's true: The sun-dried tomato cream sauce will make EVERYONE fall in love.

1 tablespoon extra-virgin olive oil

6 bone-in, skin-on chicken thighs (about 2 pounds)

Kosher salt

Freshly ground black pepper

2 cloves garlic, minced

1 tablespoon fresh thyme leaves

1 teaspoon crushed red pepper flakes

¾ cup low-sodium chicken broth

½ cup heavy cream

½ cup chopped sun-dried tomatoes

¼ cup freshly grated Parmesan

Freshly torn basil, for serving

1. Preheat oven to 375°F.

2. In a large oven-safe skillet over medium-high heat, heat oil. Season chicken generously with salt and pepper and sear, skin-side down, until golden, 4 to 5 minutes per side. Transfer chicken to a plate and pour off half the fat from skillet.

3. Return skillet to medium heat and add garlic, thyme, and red pepper flakes. Cook until fragrant, 1 minute, then stir in broth, heavy cream, sun-dried tomatoes, and Parmesan and season with more salt. Bring to a simmer, then return chicken to skillet, skin-side up.

4. Transfer skillet to oven and bake until chicken is cooked through (and juices run clear when chicken is pierced with a knife), 17 to 20 minutes.

5. Garnish with basil and serve.

 If you're a sun-dried-tomato hater (we feel you), use FRESH ONES instead. It won't have as much of a tangy kick, but it'll still make folks fall at your feet.

FIRECRACKER SALMON

TOTAL TIME: 35 MIN / SERVES 4

We love preparing one big fillet of salmon over a bed of citrus because it looks impressive and is stupid-easy to pull together: Pour over a sauce, bake for 20 minutes, and dig in.

Cooking spray

3 limes, thinly sliced

1 (1½-pound) skin-on salmon fillet

Kosher salt

Freshly ground black pepper

6 tablespoons melted butter

3 tablespoons sweet chili sauce

2 tablespoons brown sugar

Juice of 1 lime

2 cloves garlic, minced

½ teaspoon crushed red pepper flakes

Sliced green onions, for garnish

1. Preheat oven to 375°F. Line a large baking sheet with foil and grease foil with cooking spray.

2. Lay lime slices in an even layer in center of prepared baking sheet. Season salmon with salt and pepper and place salmon skin-side down on top of limes.

3. In a small bowl, whisk together melted butter, sweet chili sauce, brown sugar, lime juice, garlic, and red pepper flakes. Pour over salmon and cover with foil.

4. Bake until salmon is cooked through and flakes with a fork, 20 to 25 minutes. Switch oven to broil and broil until caramelized, 2 minutes.

5. Garnish with green onions before serving.

 This baking technique also works with LEMON or GRAPEFRUIT SLICES or PINEAPPLE RINGS.

PRIMAVERA STUFFED CHICKEN

TOTAL TIME: 40 MIN / SERVES 4

We always thought stuffing chicken was super annoying, but then we did it hasselback-style, like a baked potato, and haven't looked back. With zucchini, tomatoes, peppers, and cheese in every bite, how could you go wrong?

4 boneless, skinless chicken breasts (about 1½ pounds)

1 zucchini, halved lengthwise and thinly sliced into half-moons

3 medium tomatoes, halved and thinly sliced into half-moons

2 yellow bell peppers, thinly sliced

½ red onion, thinly sliced

2 tablespoons extra-virgin olive oil

1 teaspoon Italian seasoning

Kosher salt

Freshly ground black pepper

1 cup shredded mozzarella

Freshly chopped parsley, for garnish

1. Preheat oven to 400°F.

2. Make slits in each chicken breast, being careful not to cut through completely, and stuff with zucchini, tomatoes, bell peppers, and red onion.

3. Drizzle with oil and season with Italian seasoning, salt, and pepper. Sprinkle with mozzarella.

4. Bake until chicken is cooked through and no longer pink inside, 25 minutes.

5. Garnish with parsley before serving.

You can stuff this chicken with **ALMOST ANYTHING.** Try sliced ham, Swiss, and pickle chips, or sun-dried tomatoes, kalamata olives, and feta.

RANCH ROAST CHICKEN

TOTAL TIME: 1 HR 40 MIN / SERVES 6

Spatchcocking seems annoyingly fussy, but it's actually so simple—and it cuts cooking time by almost half. Try it once and you might never roast a whole chicken any other way.

1 (4-pound) whole chicken

4 tablespoons melted butter

½ (1-ounce) packet ranch seasoning

1 tablespoon freshly chopped chives

Kosher salt

Freshly ground black pepper

1 pound baby potatoes, halved or quartered if large

4 stalks celery, cut into 1-inch pieces

4 large carrots, sliced into 1-inch pieces

3 shallots, quartered

6 cloves garlic

2 tablespoons extra-virgin olive oil

1. Preheat oven to 425°F.

2. Place chicken, breast-side down, on a cutting board. Using kitchen shears, cut along one side of backbone starting at thigh. Turn chicken around and cut along other side. Discard backbone. Flip chicken and open it like a book. Press firmly on breastbone to flatten.

3. In a small bowl, mix together melted butter, ranch seasoning, and chives. Rub mixture all over chicken and season generously with salt and pepper.

4. On a large baking sheet, toss potatoes, celery, carrots, shallots, and garlic with oil and place chicken on top.

5. Roast until chicken is cooked through (and juices run clear when chicken is pierced with a knife) and a thermometer inserted into thickest part of breast registers 165°F, 45 to 50 minutes.

6. Remove chicken from baking sheet and let rest on a cutting board; continue baking vegetables until tender, about 20 minutes more.

7. Carve chicken and serve with roasted vegetables.

SPATCHCOCK:

v. the method of cooking a chicken by splitting it down the back and laying it flat. Also WORST WORD EVER.

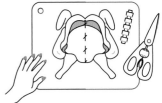

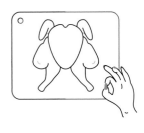

GENERAL TSO WRAPS

4 WAYS TO USE ROTISSERIE CHICKEN

1 GENERAL TSO WRAPS

In a large skillet over medium heat, heat 1 tablespoon sesame oil. Stir in 2 minced garlic cloves and 1 teaspoon minced fresh ginger and cook 1 minute. Add 1 tablespoon cornstarch and stir until coated, then add ½ cup chicken broth, ¼ cup soy sauce, 2 tablespoons apple cider vinegar, 1 tablespoon hoisin sauce, and 1 tablespoon honey. Simmer 2 minutes, then stir in 3 cups shredded rotisserie chicken. Spoon chicken onto Bibb lettuce leaves and garnish with green onions and sesame seeds.

2 CHICKEN POT PIE NOODLES

In a large skillet over medium heat, melt 2 tablespoons butter. Add 2 cubed carrots, 2 cubed stalks celery, 1 diced large onion, and 2 minced cloves garlic and season with salt and pepper. Cook until softened, 3 minutes, then stir in 2 tablespoons all-purpose flour and cook 1 minute. Stir in ½ cup each chicken broth and heavy cream and simmer, stirring occasionally, until thickened, 5 minutes. Stir in 10 ounces cooked pasta, 1½ cups shredded rotisserie chicken and ½ cup each frozen peas and corn and simmer until warmed through.

3 RANCH CHICKEN CHILI

In a large pot over medium heat, heat 1 tablespoon olive oil. Add 1 chopped medium onion and cook until soft, 5 minutes. Add 2 minced garlic cloves, 2 teaspoons dried oregano, and 2 teaspoons ranch seasoning. Cook 1 minute. Add 2 cups shredded rotisserie chicken and 3 cups chicken broth and simmer, 20 minutes. Mash 1 (15-ounce) can white beans with a fork and add to pot along with 2 (4.5-ounce) cans green chiles. Season with salt and pepper. Ladle chili into bowls and squeeze lime juice over top. Top with sour cream and cilantro.

4 BUFFALO CHICKEN TAQUITOS

In a medium bowl, mix together 2 cups shredded rotisserie chicken, ½ (8-ounce) block softened cream cheese, and ¼ cup each ranch dressing, Buffalo sauce, and crumbled blue cheese. Season with salt and pepper. Add 2 tablespoons of chicken mixture to a warm corn tortilla, then roll up. Repeat with remaining mixture. In a large skillet over medium heat, heat 2 tablespoons vegetable oil. Cook taquitos seam-side down until golden, 6 minutes.

CHICKEN PARM SOUP

TOTAL TIME: 45 MIN / SERVES 4 TO 6

No version of chicken Parm is released into the universe until it's given a stamp of approval by Lindsey (right), our on-staff chicken Parm consultant (she's tasted hundreds of versions). This soup is one of her favorites ever—which says a lot.

- 1 tablespoon extra-virgin olive oil
- 1 large onion, chopped
- 3 cloves garlic, minced
- 3 tablespoons tomato paste
- 1 teaspoon crushed red pepper flakes
- 1 (15-ounce) can diced or crushed tomatoes
- 6 cups low-sodium chicken broth

- 8 ounces penne
- ¾ pound cooked chicken breast (about 2 breasts)
- 1½ cups shredded mozzarella
- 1 cup freshly grated Parmesan
- 1 tablespoon freshly chopped parsley
- Kosher salt
- Freshly ground black pepper

1. In a large pot over medium heat, heat oil. Add onion and cook, stirring, until soft, 5 minutes. Add garlic and cook until fragrant, 1 minute more. Stir in tomato paste and red pepper flakes. Add tomatoes and broth and bring to a simmer.

2. Add penne and cook until al dente, 8 to 10 minutes.

3. Add chicken, mozzarella, Parmesan, and parsley and season generously with salt and pepper. Let cheese melt, then ladle into bowls.

SHEET PAN SHRIMP BOIL

DELISH FAVE

TOTAL TIME: 35 MIN / SERVES 4

Shrimp boil is one of those things that's actually totally annoying to make at home, which is why this sheet-pan trick is so genius: You can bake the shrimp, potatoes, corn, and sausage all at once, and there's no enormous pot to clean.

---

1 pound baby red potatoes, quartered

1½ pounds raw medium shrimp, peeled and deveined

2 ears corn, cut crosswise into 4 pieces each

2 links smoked andouille sausage, thinly sliced

2 lemons, sliced

1 teaspoon garlic powder

1 tablespoon Old Bay seasoning

2 tablespoons melted butter

2 tablespoons extra-virgin olive oil

Kosher salt

Freshly ground black pepper

Freshly chopped parsley, for garnish

Old Bay Mayo

1. Preheat oven to 425°F.

2. In a large pot of salted boiling water, cook potatoes until just tender, about 10 minutes. Drain.

3. In a large bowl, combine cooked potatoes, shrimp, corn, sausage, lemons, garlic powder, Old Bay, melted butter, and oil and season with salt and pepper. Toss until combined, then divide between two large baking sheets.

4. Bake until shrimp is cooked through and corn is tender, 13 to 15 minutes.

5. Garnish with parsley and serve with Old Bay Mayo.

OLD BAY MAYO

In a small bowl, whisk together
½ cup **MAYONNAISE**, 2 tablespoons
finely chopped fresh **CHIVES**,
1 teaspoon **OLD BAY SEASONING**,
1 teaspoon **DIJON MUSTARD**, and
juice and zest of ½ **LEMON**.

PINEAPPLE SALSA PORK CHOPS

TOTAL TIME: 35 MIN / SERVES 4

This pineapple salsa might not be better than a vacation, but it will brighten up everything from pork chops to salmon.

3 tablespoons extra-virgin olive oil

4 bone-in pork chops, fat trimmed

Kosher salt

Freshly ground black pepper

3 cups chopped pineapple

1 red bell pepper, diced

½ small red onion, chopped

4 green onions, thinly sliced

Juice of 1 lime

1. Preheat oven to 425°F. In a large oven-safe skillet over medium-high heat, heat 1 tablespoon of the oil. Season pork chops with salt and pepper and add to skillet. Sear until golden, 3 minutes per side. Transfer skillet to oven and bake until cooked through, 10 to 12 minutes.

2. Meanwhile, in a large bowl, toss pineapple, bell pepper, red and green onions, lime juice, and the 2 remaining tablespoons of the oil until combined. Season with salt and pepper.

3. Let chops rest 5 minutes, then top with pineapple salsa abefore serving.

CHEESY CHICKEN BROCCOLI BAKE

TOTAL TIME: 35 MIN / SERVES 4

This skillet casserole reminds us of broccoli cheddar cheese soup in the best way. Cooking the chicken, rice, and broccoli together in one pan lets the flavors meld.

1 tablespoon extra-virgin olive oil

1 small yellow onion, chopped

2 cloves garlic, minced

1 pound boneless, skinless chicken breasts, cut into 1-inch pieces

Kosher salt

Freshly ground black pepper

1 cup white rice

1 cup heavy cream

2½ cups low-sodium chicken broth, divided

2 cups broccoli florets

1 cup shredded cheddar cheese

¼ cup panko breadcrumbs

1. In a large oven-safe skillet over medium-high heat, heat oil. Add onion and cook, stirring, until soft, 5 minutes. Add garlic and cook until fragrant, 1 minute more. Add chicken and season with salt and pepper. Cook, stirring occasionally, until golden, about 6 minutes more.

2. Stir in rice, heavy cream, and 1 cup of the broth. Bring to a simmer and cook until rice is tender, about 15 minutes. Add remaining 1½ cups broth, broccoli, and cheddar cheese and cook until broccoli is tender and cheese is melty, about 10 minutes.

3. Preheat broiler.

4. Sprinkle chicken mixture with breadcrumbs and season with salt and pepper. Broil until golden and crispy, about 2 minutes.

BUFFALO CHICKEN CHILI

TOTAL TIME: 45 MIN / SERVES 6

The perfect game-day meal. If you're watching football and not eating this, you're doing it all wrong.

- 1 tablespoon extra-virgin olive oil
- 1 medium onion, chopped
- 2 stalks celery, chopped
- 1 teaspoon paprika
- 1 teaspoon chili powder
- ½ teaspoon ground cumin
- Kosher salt
- Freshly ground black pepper
- 2 cups low-sodium chicken broth
- 1 (15-ounce) can white beans, drained
- 1 (28-ounce) can crushed fire-roasted tomatoes
- 3 cups shredded rotisserie chicken
- ½ cup pale ale beer
- ¼ cup hot sauce, preferably Frank's RedHot
- 2 tablespoons melted butter
- Sliced green onions, for serving
- Crumbled blue cheese, for serving

1. In a large pot over medium heat, heat oil. Add onion, celery, paprika, chili powder, and cumin and season with salt and pepper. Cook, stirring, until vegetables are soft, 5 minutes.

2. Stir in broth, beans, tomatoes, chicken, beer, hot sauce, and melted butter. Bring to a simmer and cook until slightly thickened, 15 to 20 minutes. Season generously with salt and pepper and ladle into bowls.

3. Top with green onions and blue cheese before serving.

CHEESEBURGER CUPS

TOTAL TIME: 30 MIN / SERVES 4

Got picky eaters? We gotchu. This kid-approved recipe calls for pressing hamburger buns into a muffin tin to form cups, which is beyond brilliant.

Cooking spray

6 burger buns, split

1 tablespoon vegetable oil

1 medium onion, chopped

1 pound ground beef

½ teaspoon garlic powder

Kosher salt

Freshly ground black pepper

3 slices cheddar cheese, quartered

Ketchup, for serving

Yellow mustard, for serving

12 pickle chips

Sesame seeds, for garnish

1. Preheat oven to 350°F and grease a muffin tin with cooking spray.

2. Flatten burger bun halves to ¼ inch thick with a rolling pin and place one half cut-side up in each prepared muffin cup.

3. In a large skillet over medium-high heat, heat oil. Add onion and cook, stirring, until soft, about 5 minutes. Add ground beef and cook, breaking up meat with a wooden spoon, until no longer pink, about 6 minutes. Drain fat.

4. Return beef mixture to skillet and season with garlic powder, salt, and pepper. Divide ground beef mixture among burger bun cups and top each with a cheddar cheese square. Bake until cheese is melty and buns are golden, about 10 minutes.

5. Drizzle cups with ketchup and mustard, top with a pickle, and sprinkle with sesame seeds.

This burger bun trick is **ENDLESSLY ADAPTABLE:** The cups they form can be filled with anything (think: sloppy joe mix or taco meat, but don't even stop there).

BANG BANG SHRIMP

Bang Bang Sauce hits all the notes: sweet, spicy, tangy, creamy. It's perfect drizzled over breaded shrimp, but we also like dunking vegetables of all kinds into it.

2 cups panko breadcrumbs

2 tablespoons extra-virgin olive oil

1 teaspoon garlic powder

Kosher salt

Freshly ground black pepper

2 large eggs

1 cup all-purpose flour

1 pound raw shrimp, peeled and deveined

Bang Bang Sauce

Freshly chopped cilantro, for garnish

1. Preheat oven to 400°F and line a large baking sheet with parchment paper.

2. In a shallow bowl, stir together breadcrumbs, oil, and garlic powder and season with salt and pepper. In another shallow bowl, whisk eggs. Put flour in a third bowl. Using tongs, dip shrimp first in flour, then egg, then panko mixture, and transfer to prepared baking sheet. Continue until all shrimp are coated.

3. Bake until shrimp are crispy and golden, 13 to 15 minutes.

4. Drizzle Bang Bang Sauce over shrimp and garnish with cilantro before serving.

BANG BANG SAUCE

In a medium bowl, whisk together 2 tablespoons
MAYONNAISE, 2 tablespoons **SWEET CHILI SAUCE**,
1 tablespoon **SRIRACHA**, juice of 1 **LIME**, and
1 teaspoon **HONEY** and season with **SALT**.

BUFFALO CHICKEN MEATBALLS

TOTAL TIME: 30 MIN / SERVES 4

A lot of editors believe these are the best meatballs we've ever made. Consider doubling the sauce of butter, hot sauce, and blue cheese—you'll want to drink it.

Extra-virgin olive oil, for baking sheet

4 tablespoons butter

⅓ cup hot sauce, preferably Frank's RedHot

⅓ cup crumbled blue cheese

Kosher salt

⅓ cup panko breadcrumbs

2 stalks celery, finely chopped

2 cloves garlic, minced

1 large egg

¼ cup sliced green onions, plus more for garnish

½ teaspoon onion powder

1 pound ground chicken

1. Preheat oven to 425°F and brush a large baking sheet with oil.

2. In a small saucepan over medium heat, combine butter, hot sauce, and blue cheese, and season with salt. Whisk until butter and cheese have melted, 2 minutes. Remove from heat and let cool.

3. Meanwhile, in a medium bowl, stir together breadcrumbs, celery, garlic, egg, green onions, and onion powder and season with salt. Add chicken and half the hot sauce mixture and mix until combined.

4. Using a cookie scoop, form 1-inch meatballs and transfer to prepared baking sheet.

5. Bake until lightly golden, 15 to 17 minutes.

6. Drizzle remaining sauce over meatballs and sprinkle with green onions before serving.

DELISH GOES TO . . .
MINNESOTA STATE FAIR

As far as state fairs go, there's no place like Minnesota. Texas may have the highest attendance overall, but if you want to try the most over-the-top, deep-fried, skewered-on-a-stick foods, you've got to hit up the Twin Cities. Held halfway between Minneapolis and St. Paul, the fair features a rotating list of new vendors and dishes each year—which is the reason we keep going back. Here are some of our favorites.

DELISH DIARY

Texas Tater
Dogs

Deep-Fried Baklava

"Call It Breakfast" Sundae ⟶

Reuben
Pickle ⟶
Dogs

⟵ Deep-Fried Ribs

MEET THE COOKIE QUEEN!

Everywhere you walk at the Minnesota State Fair, there's a trail of chocolate chip cookie crumbs. Some smashed, some whole, all leading back to one person: Martha Rossini Olson. Since 1979, she's run the fair's most successful stand, alongside her husband, Gary, and business partner, Neil O'Leary. In a world where everything's deep-fried and served on a stick, Olson's shop stands out for kicking it old school. In twelve days, Olson racks up a cool $3 million across her three stands, which sell one thing: chocolate chip cookies. Served warm, the overflowing buckets of cookies—four dozen in each—turn customers into walking advertisements. "We wanted it to be something people had to hold, that other people would see," Olson said.

The tactic worked, creating lines so many people deep it looks more like a swarm in front of each of her three stands. Together they bake about 30,000 cookies every twelve minutes. It's a sweet job, and Olson's just the person to do it.

WATCH US MAKE 'EM
THEN WE BAKE 'EM

CHAPTER SIX

YOU WANNA PIZZA THIS?

Make it a **BOLOGNESE PIE** by swapping out the marinara for your favorite meat sauce and skipping the sliced pepperoni.

PIZZA RIGATONI PIE

TOTAL TIME: 1 HR / SERVES 6

The gasps when this thing comes out of the oven are a testament to its power—who knew pasta could turn into something so sculptural?! This recipe should be a family affair: It's totally satisfying and weirdly fun to build.

12 ounces rigatoni

2 tablespoons extra-virgin olive oil, divided

1½ cups shredded mozzarella, divided

½ cup freshly grated Parmesan, divided

2 cups ricotta

2 large eggs

2 tablespoons milk (preferably whole or 2%)

Kosher salt

Freshly ground black pepper

1 (13-ounce) jar pizza sauce or marinara, divided

¼ cup sliced pepperoni

Freshly sliced basil, for garnish

1. Preheat oven to 400°F.

2. In a large pot of salted boiling water, cook rigatoni until very al dente, about 8 minutes. Drain and rinse with cold water. Transfer to a large bowl with 1 tablespoon of oil, ½ cup of mozzarella, and ¼ cup of Parmesan and stir to combine.

3. In a small bowl, combine ricotta, eggs, and milk and season with salt and pepper.

4. Build pie: Brush a 9-inch springform pan with remaining 1 tablespoon oil and wrap bottom of pan in foil. Spread bottom and edges of pan with ¼ cup of pizza sauce. Stand rigatoni upright in pan **A**, tightly packing it in to fill pan. Spoon over ricotta mixture and spread with a spatula, pressing down to fill tubes **B**. Spoon over remaining pizza sauce, creating an even layer **C**. Top rigatoni with remaining 1 cup mozzarella and ¼ cup Parmesan, then with pepperoni **D**.

5. Bake until deeply golden and bubbly, 30 minutes.

6. Garnish with basil before serving.

WATCH & LEARN

A B C D

159

WELCOME TO PIZZA LOUNGE!

When you're creating a brand as delightful as Delish, a **normal** conference room just doesn't cut it. Enter Pizza Lounge, our meeting space where form and function are replaced by **whimsy** and comfort. The chairs are replaced by food-themed **bean bags**, the couch has **cup holders**, and the wall is appropriately aggressive ("You wanna pizza me?"). If the **neon pizza sign** in the window doesn't alert the passing public to where we sit in the Hearst Tower, we don't know what will.

PIZZA PINWHEELS

TOTAL TIME: 55 MIN / SERVES 8

Imagine taking a pizza, rolling the whole thing up, and slicing it into rounds cinnamon bun–style—that's basically what this recipe is. If the crust is your favorite part of the pizza, you'll live for these.

Cooking spray

All-purpose flour, for rolling dough

1 pound refrigerated pizza dough, halved

2 cups shredded mozzarella, divided

1 cup sliced pepperoni

3 tablespoons extra-virgin olive oil

1 tablespoon freshly chopped parsley

1 teaspoon garlic powder

Kosher salt

¼ cup freshly grated Parmesan, plus more for garnish

Pizza sauce, warmed, for dipping

1. Preheat oven to 425°F and grease a 9x9-inch pan with cooking spray.

2. On a lightly floured surface, roll out half of pizza dough into a large rectangle. (Cover second piece of dough with dishtowel until ready to use.) Top with half of mozzarella and pepperoni. Starting with long end closest to you, tightly roll pizza dough into a spiral.

3. Using a sharp knife, cut roll in half crosswise, then slice each of the halves into 1-inch-thick pinwheels. Place pinwheels cut-side up in prepared pan, making sure they're touching. Repeat process with remaining pizza dough, mozzarella, and pepperoni.

4. In a small bowl, whisk together oil, parsley, and garlic powder and season with salt. Brush mixture over tops of pinwheels and sprinkle with Parmesan.

5. Bake until dough is golden and cheese is melty, 22 to 25 minutes.

6. Sprinkle with Parmesan and serve with pizza sauce.

PIZZA POT PIE

TOTAL TIME: 1 HR 10 MIN / SERVES 4

TBH, this was an idea that got blurted out in a meeting, and we had no idea where to start. But it kind of makes sense—it's sort of like an upside-down deep-dish: The crust is on top, and the center is filled with Italian sausage, mushrooms, and peppers.

2 tablespoons extra-virgin olive oil, plus more for crust

2 cups broccoli florets, roughly chopped

2 bell peppers, diced

8 ounces sliced mushrooms

1 pound Italian sausage (sweet or spicy), casings removed

¼ cup all-purpose flour, plus more for rolling dough

2 cloves garlic, minced

1 teaspoon dried oregano

Kosher salt

Freshly ground black pepper

2 cups pizza sauce

½ pound refrigerated pizza dough

2 cups shredded mozzarella

¼ cup sliced pepperoni

Freshly grated Parmesan, for garnish

Freshly chopped parsley, for garnish

1. Preheat oven to 400°F.

2. In a 10- or 12-inch oven-safe skillet over medium heat, heat oil. Add broccoli and bell peppers and cook, stirring often, until slightly soft, 5 minutes. Add mushrooms and cook, stirring, until soft, 4 minutes more.

3. Add sausage and cook, breaking it up with a wooden spoon, until seared and no longer pink, about 4 minutes. Add flour and stir until vegetables and sausage are well coated, then add garlic and oregano and season with salt and pepper. Stir in pizza sauce and remove from heat. Let cool 10 minutes.

4. On a lightly floured surface, roll out pizza dough into a large circle a couple inches bigger than your skillet. Top sausage mixture with mozzarella, then place dough round over skillet and carefully crimp edges. Brush with oil and top with pepperoni.

5. Bake until crust is golden, about 40 minutes.

6. Let cool 10 minutes, then sprinkle with Parmesan and parsley before serving.

PIZZADILLA

TOTAL TIME: 30 MIN / MAKES 1

Quesadillas are the kind of food you don't really need a recipe for—how hard is it to throw cheese into a tortilla? A PIZZAdilla, on the other hand, needs to be explained to be believed. It's all your favorite pizza elements stuffed in the inside and layered on the outside.

1 tablespoon extra-virgin olive oil

2 medium flour tortillas

⅓ cup pizza sauce

2 cloves garlic, minced

1 cup shredded mozzarella

½ cup freshly grated Parmesan

⅓ cup sliced pepperoni

¼ teaspoon Italian seasoning

Freshly chopped parsley, for garnish

1. Preheat broiler.

2. In a large oven-safe skillet over medium heat, heat oil. Add one tortilla to skillet and spread about half of pizza sauce on top. Scatter garlic on top and sprinkle with half of mozzarella, Parmesan, pepperoni, and Italian seasoning.

3. Top with second tortilla and cook until cheese is melty and tortilla is golden.

4. When ready to flip, cover skillet with a large plate and invert skillet to transfer quesadilla onto plate, then slide quesadilla back into skillet, cooked-side up. Top with remaining pizza sauce, mozzarella, Parmesan, pepperoni, and Italian seasoning.

5. Place skillet under broiler and broil until cheese is melty and pepperoni are crispy, about 2 minutes.

6. Garnish with parsley before serving.

ANY PIZZA IS A

PERSONAL PIZZA IF YOU

BELIEVE IN YOURSELF

PIZZA STUFFED BREAD

TOTAL TIME: 40 MIN / SERVES 6

Getting the perfect "cheese pull" on camera is a rite of passage at Delish—and we'll do pretty much anything to get it right. The first time we made this for a photo shoot, we needed to get the pull while the bread was scalding hot. Imagine us pulling, screaming, and then immediately dunking our fingers in ice water. In real life, wait a few minutes before you serve it.

1 large boule

½ cup (1 stick) melted butter

2 cloves garlic, minced

¼ cup freshly grated Parmesan

2 tablespoons freshly chopped parsley

Kosher salt

Freshly ground black pepper

1 cup pizza sauce

2 cups shredded mozzarella

⅓ cup sliced mini pepperoni (or diced pepperoni)

1. Preheat oven to 350°F and line a large baking sheet with parchment paper.

2. Using a serrated knife, crosshatch boule, slicing every inch in both directions and making sure to not slice through the bottom (see page 368).

3. In a small bowl, whisk together melted butter, garlic, Parmesan, and parsley and season with salt and pepper. Brush insides of bread with butter mixture, making sure to get it into crosshatches.

4. Spoon pizza sauce into crosshatches, then stuff with mozzarella and pepperoni. Sprinkle whole loaf with remaining mozzarella and pepperoni.

5. Bake until cheese is melty and bread is toasted, about 20 minutes.

6. Let cool 5 minutes before serving.

PIZZA WAFFLES

TOTAL TIME: 25 MIN / MAKES 4

The waffle iron is having such a moment right now (we've crammed everything we can think of into it). But nothing has blown our minds more than this: refrigerated biscuit dough layered with sauce and cheese, and then waffled. It's upsettingly perfect.

Cooking spray

1 (16.3-ounce) can refrigerated biscuits

2 cups shredded mozzarella

¼ cup pizza sauce

1 cup sliced mini pepperoni

Freshly grated Parmesan, for garnish

1. Heat waffle iron and grease with cooking spray.

2. Using your hands or a rolling pin, roll out biscuits into flat patties. Top half of biscuits with ½ cup of mozzarella and 1 tablespoon of pizza sauce, then sprinkle with pepperoni. Top each with a second biscuit and seal edges.

3. Working one at a time, cook waffles until golden and cooked through, about 3 minutes.

4. Sprinkle with Parmesan and cut into wedges.

EXTREME DEEP-DISH PIZZA

LOU MALNATI'S / Chicago, IL

If you judge a pizza by its cheese pull, Lou Malnati's has the competition beat: Chicago's famous deep-dish joint tops its pies with so much mozzarella, every slice grabbed is a Boomerang waiting to happen. The fifty or so Windy City locations are the kind of place your diet goes to die, since just one of those slices clocks in at around 700 calories. Don't blame it all on the mozz, though. There's Italian sausage, crushed tomatoes, and a sprinkle of herbs and Parm, too. Even the crust is epic: Nearly two pounds of dough are used for every pie, and Malnati's has the stuff trademarked. (It's called Buttercrust—an obvious nod to the crust's buttery flavor.) All in, the pie takes half an hour to bake through. But for true deep-dish fans, the wait is worth it, apparently: Malnati's sells 3 million pizzas every year.

5 WAYS TO USE PIZZA DOUGH

TOO-MUCH-BUTTER GARLIC KNOTS

1

TOO-MUCH-BUTTER GARLIC KNOTS

On a lightly floured surface, divide 2 pounds refrigerated pizza dough into 4 balls, then divide each ball into 3 strips. Roll out and stretch each into a 10-inch-long strip and tie into a knot. Transfer to a parchment-lined baking sheet. In a bowl, stir together 1 cup melted butter, 2 tablespoons chopped parsley, 2 teaspoons garlic powder, and a pinch kosher salt. Brush all over garlic knots. Bake at 425°F, brushing with melted butter mixture every 10 minutes, until golden, 30 minutes. Sprinkle with grated Parmesan.

2

CHICKEN BAKE

On a lightly floured surface, divide 1 pound refrigerated pizza dough into 2 balls and roll and stretch until ¼ inch thick. Top each with 2 tablespoons Caesar dressing, ½ cup chopped cooked chicken breast, ½ cup chopped cooked bacon, 1 cup shredded mozzarella, ¼ cup grated Parmesan, and sliced green onions. Roll pizza dough, like a cinnamon roll, into two large logs. Transfer to a large parchment-lined baking sheet and brush with egg wash. Sprinkle with more cheese and Italian seasoning. Bake at 425°F until golden, 25 minutes.

3

CHEESY RANCH BREADSTICKS

On a lightly floured surface, roll out 1 pound refrigerated pizza dough into a large oval and transfer to a parchment-lined baking sheet. Brush with olive oil and sprinkle with ½ (1-ounce) packet ranch seasoning. Cut dough crosswise into 12 long strips, then cut in half vertically. Sprinkle all over with 1 cup shredded Monterey jack cheese and chopped chives. Bake at 425°F until golden, 15 minutes. Serve with ranch dressing.

4

SOFT PRETZEL BITES

On a lightly floured surface, divide 1 pound refrigerated pizza dough into 4 pieces and roll into skinny 14-inch-long ropes. Cut each rope into twelve 1-inch pieces. Bring 4 cups water to a boil in a large pot. Stir in ¼ cup baking soda until dissolved, then reduce heat to a simmer and cook dough, in batches, until puffy and shiny, 30 seconds. Transfer with a slotted spoon to a parchment-lined baking sheet. Brush dough with 2 tablespoons melted butter and sprinkle with coarse salt. Bake at 400°F until golden, 15 minutes. Serve with mustard.

5

MEATBALL CUPS

In a large bowl, mix 1 pound ground beef, ¼ cup finely chopped onion, ¼ cup panko breadcrumbs, 1 minced clove garlic, 2 tablespoons freshly chopped parsley, and 1 large egg until combined, then shape into 24 meatballs. On a lightly floured surface, halve 1 pound refrigerated pizza dough, then cut each half into 12 pieces (24 total). Roll each into a thin circle, then nestle into a greased mini-muffin tin and add a meatball to each muffin cup. Top each with a spoonful of marinara, shredded mozzarella, and grated Parmesan and brush dough with olive oil. Bake at 400°F until golden and cooked through, about 22 minutes.

DELISH FAVE

BACON
PICKLE
PIZZA

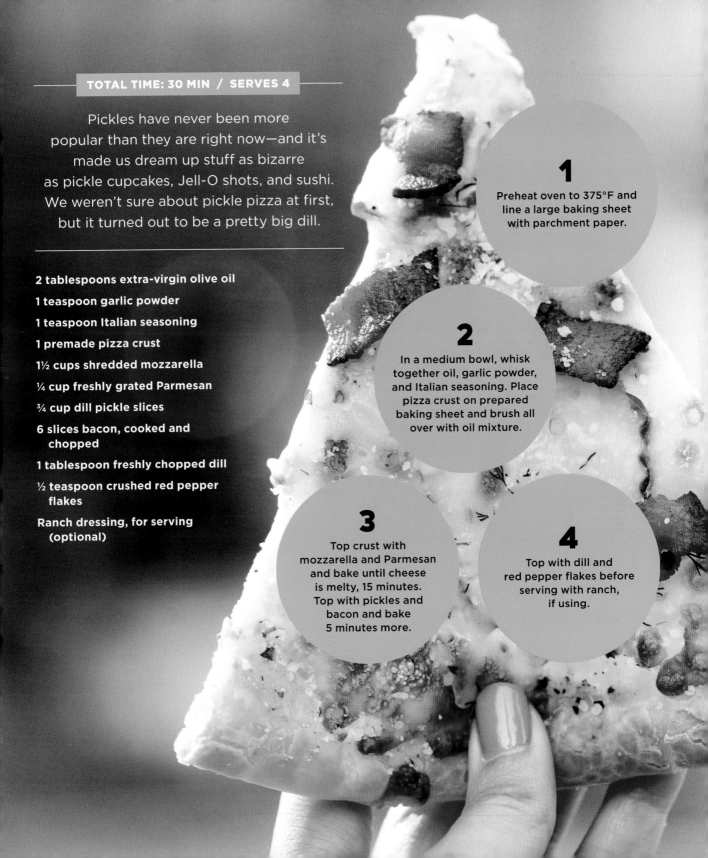

TOTAL TIME: 30 MIN / SERVES 4

Pickles have never been more popular than they are right now—and it's made us dream up stuff as bizarre as pickle cupcakes, Jell-O shots, and sushi. We weren't sure about pickle pizza at first, but it turned out to be a pretty big dill.

2 tablespoons extra-virgin olive oil

1 teaspoon garlic powder

1 teaspoon Italian seasoning

1 premade pizza crust

1½ cups shredded mozzarella

¼ cup freshly grated Parmesan

¾ cup dill pickle slices

6 slices bacon, cooked and chopped

1 tablespoon freshly chopped dill

½ teaspoon crushed red pepper flakes

Ranch dressing, for serving (optional)

1
Preheat oven to 375°F and line a large baking sheet with parchment paper.

2
In a medium bowl, whisk together oil, garlic powder, and Italian seasoning. Place pizza crust on prepared baking sheet and brush all over with oil mixture.

3
Top crust with mozzarella and Parmesan and bake until cheese is melty, 15 minutes. Top with pickles and bacon and bake 5 minutes more.

4
Top with dill and red pepper flakes before serving with ranch, if using.

PIZZAGNA

TOTAL TIME: 1 HR 55 MIN / SERVES 8

This recipe was actually inspired by a version we saw in our cafeteria in the Hearst Tower—we immediately fell for the genius recipe name. Pepperoni and a traditional meat sauce combine into the sexiest lasagna ever.

1 pound lasagna noodles

1 tablespoon extra-virgin olive oil, plus more for noodles

½ large onion, chopped

8 ounces sliced white mushrooms

1 pound ground beef

1 tablespoon dried oregano

¼ teaspoon crushed red pepper flakes

1 (32-ounce) jar marinara

Kosher salt

2 (15-ounce) containers whole-milk ricotta

2 large eggs

1 cup freshly grated Parmesan

Freshly ground black pepper

1 cup sliced pepperoni

3 cups shredded mozzarella

Freshly chopped parsley, for garnish

1. Preheat oven to 375°F.

2. In a large pot of salted boiling water, cook lasagna noodles according to package directions until al dente. Drain and transfer to a baking sheet to cool. Toss with a splash of oil to prevent sticking, and set aside.

3. In a large skillet over medium-high heat, heat oil. Add onion and mushrooms and cook, stirring, until soft, about 5 minutes. Add ground beef and cook, breaking up with a wooden spoon, until no longer pink, about 8 minutes. Drain fat. Return beef mixture to skillet over medium heat and stir in oregano, red pepper flakes, and marinara and season with salt. Simmer 10 minutes.

4. In a medium bowl, stir together ricotta, eggs, and Parmesan and season with salt and pepper.

5. Assemble lasagna: Spread a thin layer of meat sauce in a large baking dish and top with a layer of 4 overlapping noodles. Spread a layer of ricotta mixture over noodle layer, sprinkle with a layer of mozzarella and pepperoni, and top with more sauce. Repeat three more times, topping the final layer of noodles with ricotta, then sauce, mozzarella, and pepperoni.

6. Tent with foil and bake 35 minutes. Remove foil and bake until golden, 10 minutes more.

7. Let cool 15 minutes, then garnish with parsley before serving.

VEGGIE SUPREME CAULI PIZZA

TOTAL TIME: 1 HR 10 MIN / SERVES 4

We'd be lying if we said cauli crust holds its own against the real thing, but this can totally satisfy even the most psychotic pizza addict. Make sure you use some muscle when draining the cauli—a soggy crust really sucks.

Cooking spray

1 large head cauliflower, grated, or 4 cups riced cauliflower

1 large egg

2 cups shredded mozzarella, divided

½ cup freshly grated Parmesan, divided

2 cloves garlic, minced

Kosher salt

⅓ cup pizza sauce or marinara

1 yellow bell pepper, diced

½ cup chopped broccoli florets

¼ small red onion, thinly sliced

¼ cup sliced black olives

1. Preheat oven to 425°F. Grease a large baking sheet with cooking spray.

2. Put grated cauliflower in a clean dishtowel and twist to drain excess liquid. Transfer cauliflower to a large bowl and add egg, 1 cup of mozzarella, ¼ cup of Parmesan, and garlic and season with salt. Stir until everything is moist and combined.

3. Transfer cauliflower mixture to prepared baking sheet and pat into a thin crust. Pat with paper towels to soak up any liquid.

4. Bake until golden and dried out, 20 minutes.

5. Top crust with pizza sauce, remaining 1 cup mozzarella, remaining ¼ cup Parmesan, bell pepper, broccoli, onion, and olives and bake until vegetables are tender and crust is crisp, 10 to 12 minutes more.

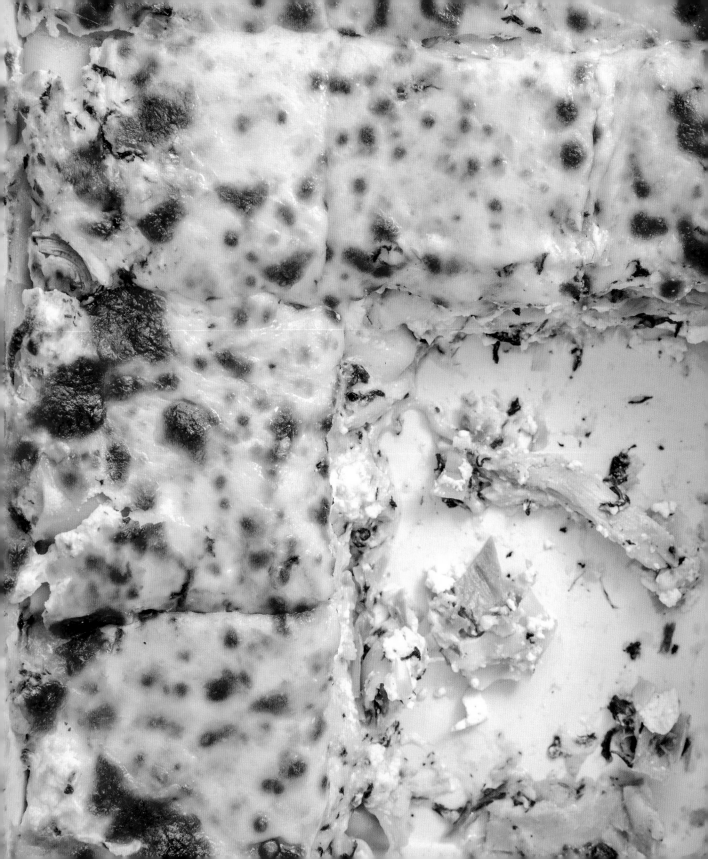

CHAPTER SEVEN

CARB YOUR ENTHUSIASM

Pastas, noodles, and more.

TUSCAN CHICKEN PASTA

TOTAL TIME: 45 MIN / SERVES 4

This is the pasta that put us on the map: We developed this recipe our first Valentine's Day and people went CRAZY for it. The chicken-bacon combo makes it feel special enough for date night, but we know people who make it every single week.

12 ounces spaghetti or angel hair pasta

1 tablespoon extra-virgin olive oil

3 boneless, skinless chicken breasts (about 1¼ pounds)

Kosher salt

Freshly ground black pepper

6 slices bacon

2 cloves garlic, minced

2 cups diced tomatoes (fresh or canned)

3 cups baby spinach

½ cup heavy cream

⅓ cup freshly grated Parmesan

Freshly torn basil, for garnish

1. In a large pot of salted boiling water, cook pasta according to package directions until al dente. Drain, reserving 1 cup pasta water.

2. Meanwhile, in a large skillet over medium-high heat, heat oil. Season chicken with salt and pepper and cook until golden and no longer pink inside, about 8 minutes per side. Let rest 10 minutes, then thinly slice.

3. Meanwhile, in same skillet, cook bacon over medium heat until crispy, 8 minutes. Drain on a paper towel–lined plate, then chop. Pour off half of fat from skillet.

4. Add garlic, tomatoes, and spinach to skillet and cook over medium heat until fragrant and slightly wilted, 2 minutes. Season with salt and pepper, then add heavy cream, Parmesan, and ½ cup of reserved pasta water. Simmer 5 minutes.

5. Add cooked pasta and toss until fully coated, then add chicken and bacon and toss until combined. (For a looser sauce, stir in more reserved pasta water.)

6. Garnish with basil before serving.

ITALIAN MAC & CHEESE

In the beginning, there were only five of us—and on that day long ago when this recipe came out of the oven, we knew we were all soul mates when we gathered around it, forks in hand, and ate the entire thing. It's more of a cheater's mac & cheese: You don't make a béchamel or bother with breadcrumbs, and you cook the pasta right in the sauce.

1 pound Italian sausage (hot or sweet), casings removed

1 large onion, diced

2 cloves garlic, minced

1 red bell pepper, diced

12 ounces cavatappi pasta

1 (16-ounce) jar marinara

4 cups low-sodium chicken broth

Kosher salt

¼ cup half-and-half or heavy cream

2 cups shredded mozzarella, divided

Freshly chopped parsley, for garnish

1. Preheat oven to 350°F

2. In a large oven-safe skillet over medium-high heat, cook sausage, breaking up with a wooden spoon, until seared and no longer pink, about 4 minutes. Add onion, garlic, and bell pepper and cook, stirring, until soft, 5 minutes more.

3. Add cavatappi and stir until coated, then pour over marinara and broth and season with salt. Bring liquid to a boil, then reduce heat to medium-low and simmer until pasta is al dente and almost all liquid has been absorbed, about 25 minutes.

4. Stir in half-and-half and simmer until mostly absorbed, 2 minutes more. Remove from heat and stir in half of mozzarella.

5. Transfer mixture to a large baking dish and sprinkle with remaining mozzarella. Bake until cheese is bubbly and golden, about 10 minutes.

6. Garnish with parsley before serving.

BEEF & BROCCOLI NOODLES

TOTAL TIME: 45 MIN / SERVES 4

Our readers love these noodles—the photo alone is enough to motivate hundreds of thousands of comments. The Sriracha-soy-lime sauce is scary addictive, so consider yourself warned.

12 ounces wide rice noodles or udon noodles

⅓ cup low-sodium soy sauce

3 cloves garlic, minced

Juice of 1 lime, plus wedges for serving

1 tablespoon Sriracha

1 tablespoon honey

3 tablespoons toasted sesame oil, divided

1 tablespoon cornstarch

¾ pound flank steak, thinly sliced against the grain

1 large head broccoli, cut into florets

8 ounces baby bella mushrooms, sliced

1. In a large pot of salted boiling water, cook noodles according to package directions until al dente. Drain, then rinse with cold water.

2. In a small bowl, whisk together soy sauce, garlic, lime juice, Sriracha, honey, and 2 tablespoons of sesame oil, then whisk in cornstarch until smooth.

3. In a large skillet over medium-high heat, heat remaining 1 tablespoon sesame oil. Add steak and sear 3 to 5 minutes per side.

4. Stir in broccoli, mushrooms, and 2 tablespoons water and cook until tender, about 6 minutes more. Add sauce, simmer 3 minutes, then reduce heat to low and add cooked noodles. Toss until fully coated and warmed through.

5. Serve with lime wedges.

 THIS SAUCE IS BOSS . . . so use it whenever you can: on roasted Brussels sprouts, over baked salmon, or with chicken tenders.

CREAMY THREE-CHEESE SPAGHETTI

TOTAL TIME: 20 MIN / SERVES 4

Bookmark this pasta for a bad day: a breakup, an annoying email from your boss, a fight with your sister. Whatever the BS, a bowl of this can cure it. And the best part: It's Internet famous for its stupid simplicity, so it requires little to no brain power.

12 ounces spaghetti

1 tablespoon extra-virgin olive oil

3 cloves garlic, minced

¾ cup heavy cream

¾ cup low-sodium chicken broth

¾ cup shredded Italian cheese blend

Kosher salt

Freshly ground black pepper

Freshly chopped chives, for garnish

1. In a large pot of salted boiling water, cook spaghetti according to package directions until al dente. Drain, reserving 1 cup pasta water.

2. Meanwhile, in a large skillet over medium heat, heat oil. Add garlic and cook until fragrant, 1 minute, then add heavy cream, broth, and ½ cup of reserved pasta water. Add cooked spaghetti and toss until noodles are fully coated and liquid is simmering.

3. Remove from heat and stir in cheese. Toss constantly, adding more pasta water until sauce reaches desired consistency. Season with salt and pepper and garnish with chives before serving.

This pasta is a blank canvas . . . and while it's absolute perfection plain, you can totally mix in things like SAUTEED SHRIMP, GRILLED SKIRT STEAK, or COOKED CHORIZO.

AVOCADO PESTO LINGUINE

TOTAL TIME: 25 MIN / SERVES 4

Life hack: Avocado makes the most delicious pesto EVER. The creamy texture replaces the need for Parm, so it's completely dairy-free.

12 ounces linguine

1 avocado

2 cups fresh basil leaves

⅓ cup extra-virgin olive oil

Juice of ½ lemon

¼ cup pine nuts, toasted

Kosher salt

1 cup grape or cherry tomatoes, halved

1. In a large pot of salted boiling water, cook linguine according to package directions until al dente. Drain, reserving 1 cup pasta water.

2. Meanwhile, in a food processor, blend avocado, basil, oil, lemon juice, and pine nuts until creamy. (For a looser texture, add another splash of oil.) Season with salt.

3. In a large bowl, toss pesto, linguine, ½ cup reserved pasta water, and tomatoes until combined. (For a looser sauce, stir in more reserved pasta water.)

IT'S A SNAP!

HOW-TO

COOK PASTA FASTER

Patience may be a virtue, but it won't get your pasta from pot to plate in record time. That is, however, the promise of this hack: Reach for a frying pan instead of a pot. Put your pasta in the pan, then pour enough cold water on top to cover the noodles by half an inch. Turn your burner to medium-high heat and stir occasionally. The noodles will cook in about 10 minutes—and you won't have to watch a pot come to a boil.

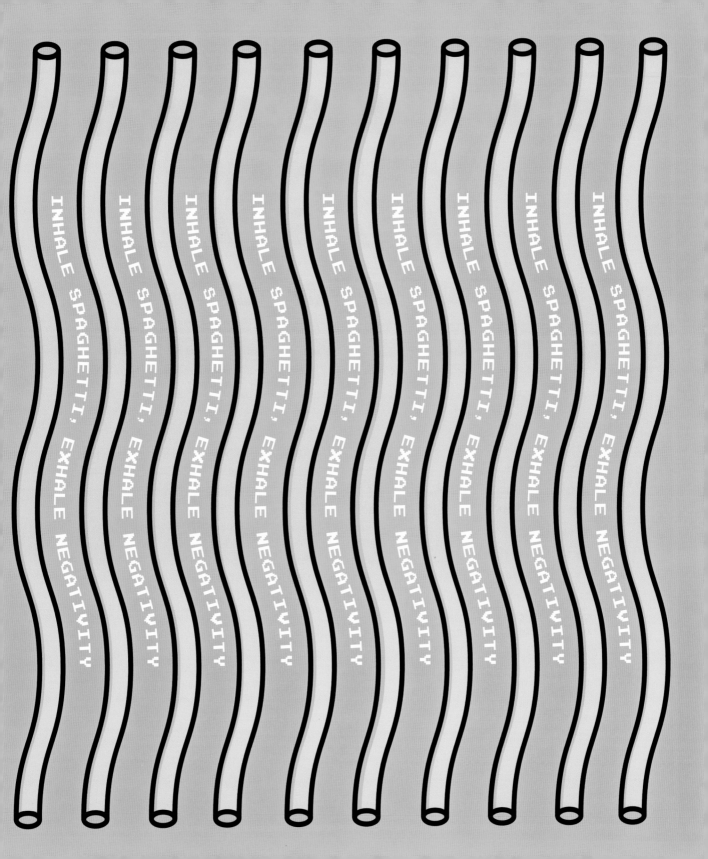

CHICKEN SPINACH ARTICHOKE LASAGNA

TOTAL TIME: 1 HR 15 MIN / SERVES 8

The perfect dinner party recipe for those of us who are somewhat reluctant to grow up. The lasagna says, "I'm an adult!" The spinach and artichoke dip that's layered inside says, "But I also really like to party!"

1 pound lasagna noodles

3 tablespoons butter

2 cloves garlic, minced

3 tablespoons all-purpose flour

3 cups milk (preferably whole or 2%)

Kosher salt

Freshly ground black pepper

1 cup freshly grated Parmesan

2 cups shredded rotisserie chicken

½ pound frozen chopped spinach, thawed and squeezed of excess liquid

1 (15-ounce) can artichoke hearts, drained and chopped

2 (15-ounce) containers part-skim ricotta

4 cups shredded mozzarella

1. Preheat oven to 350°F.

2. In a large pot of salted boiling water, cook lasagna noodles according to package directions until al dente. Drain and transfer to a baking sheet to cool.

3. Meanwhile, in a large skillet over medium heat, melt butter. Add garlic and cook until fragrant, 1 minute, then add flour and cook 1 minute more. Pour over milk and season with salt and pepper. Bring to a simmer and let thicken, 2 to 4 minutes. Add Parmesan and stir until creamy, then add rotisserie chicken, chopped spinach, and artichokes and stir until combined.

4. Assemble lasagna: Spread a thin layer of chicken mixture in a large baking dish and top with a layer of overlapping noodles. Spread a layer of ricotta over the noodles, add a layer of chicken mixture, and sprinkle with a layer of mozzarella. Repeat for three layers total, ending with mozzarella.

5. Tent with foil and bake 35 minutes. Remove foil and bake until browned and bubbly, 10 minutes more.

6. Let cool 15 minutes before slicing and serving.

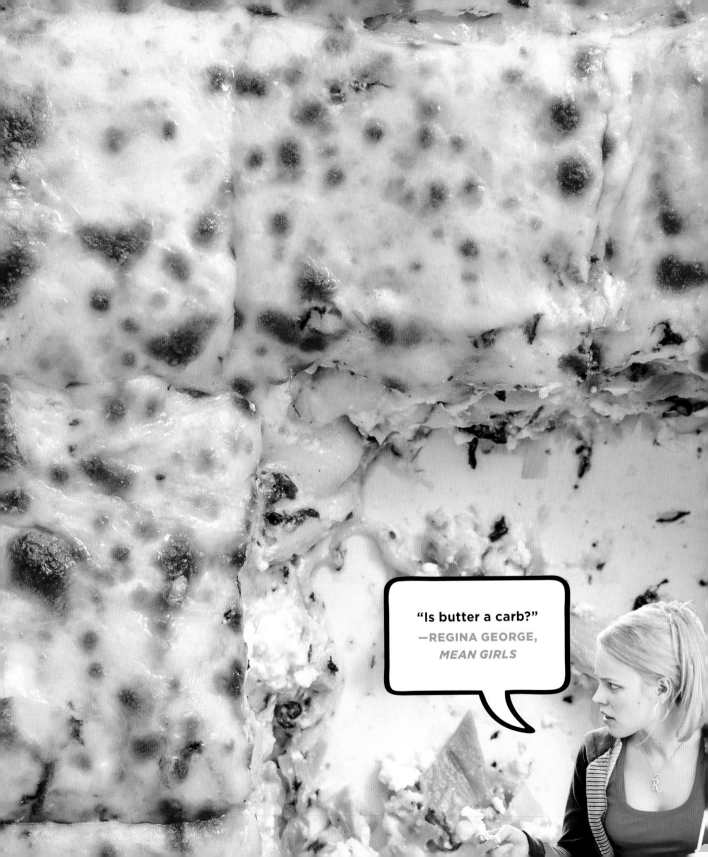

GARLICKY SHRIMP ALFREDO BAKE

TOTAL TIME: 25 MIN / SERVES 4

This recipe video is still our most viewed of all time for a reason: The shrimp, Alfredo sauce, and mozz combine all your favorite flavors.

12 ounces penne

3 tablespoons butter, divided

3 cloves garlic, minced

1 pound raw medium or large shrimp, peeled and deveined

2 tablespoons freshly chopped parsley, plus more for garnish

Kosher salt

2 tablespoons all-purpose flour

¾ cup milk (preferably whole or 2%)

¼ cup low-sodium chicken broth

1 cup shredded mozzarella, divided

¼ cup plus 2 tablespoons freshly grated Parmesan, divided

Freshly ground black pepper

1 cup chopped tomatoes (2 large)

1. Preheat oven to 350°F.

2. In a large pot of salted boiling water, cook penne according to package directions until al dente. Drain.

3. Meanwhile, in a large oven-safe skillet over medium heat, melt 1 tablespoon of butter. Add garlic, shrimp, and parsley and season with salt. Cook until shrimp is pink and no longer opaque, 2 minutes per side. Transfer shrimp to a plate. (Keep juices in skillet.)

4. Add remaining 2 tablespoons butter to skillet and let melt, then stir in flour and cook 1 minute. Add milk and broth and bring to a simmer. Stir in ¾ cup of mozzarella and ¼ cup of Parmesan and season with salt and pepper.

5. Add shrimp, tomatoes, and cooked penne and toss until combined. (Add another splash of milk if mixture is too thick.)

6. Sprinkle with remaining ¼ cup mozzarella and 2 tablespoons Parmesan and bake until melty, 5 to 7 minutes.

7. Garnish with parsley before serving.

31 MIX-INS FOR BOXED MAC & CHEESE

Some nights, cooking up a box of mac is all we can handle, too.
Upgrade it instantly with these add-ons.

**FLAMIN' HOT
CHEETOS MAC**

1 FLAMIN' HOT CHEETOS

2 BACON + BRIE

3 SLICED PEPPERONI + BASIL

4 CARAMELIZED ONIONS + BABY SPINACH

5 PIMENTO CHEESE + CRUSHED RITZ

6 SPINACH DIP + PARMESAN

7 PESTO + CHERRY TOMATOES

8 RANCH DRESSING + SHREDDED CHCKEN

9 PICKLED JALAPEÑOS + SALSA

10 BUFFALO SAUCE + BLUE CHEESE

11 SAUTÉED MUSHROOMS + STEAK SAUCE

12 AVOCADO + COTIJA

13 HOT DOGS + GREEN ONIONS

14 SUN-DRIED TOMATOES + FETA

15 GOAT CHEESE + ROSEMARY

16 BALSAMIC GLAZE + PROSCIUTTO

17 ROASTED RED PEPPERS + BLACK OLIVES

18 BROCCOLI + CHORIZO + CHIVES

19 SMOKED SALMON + DILL

20 CANNED CHILI + GROUND BEEF

21 ROASTED CAULIFLOWER + BREADCRUMBS

22 TATER TOTS + SRIRACHA

23 CHICKEN NUGGETS + MARINARA + PARMESAN

24 SLICED KIELBASA + GRUYERE

25 SHREDDED CHICKEN + BARBECUE SAUCE

26 PASTRAMI + SAUERKRAUT + RUSSIAN DRESSING

27 ROASTED BRUSSELS SPROUTS

28 LUMP CRABMEAT + ARTICHOKE HEARTS

> "Bless this highly nutritious microwaveable macaroni and cheese dinner and the people who sold it on sale."
> —KEVIN MCCALLISTER, *HOME ALONE*

29 CHIPOTLE CHILES IN ADOBO SAUCE

30 PICKLES + BACON

31 PUMPKIN PUREE + SAGE

Is the oil **HOT ENOUGH?** Flick just a few drops of water into the pan; if it sizzles, you're good.

FRIED LASAGNA

TOTAL TIME: 50 MIN / MAKES 10

Most people go to Olive Garden for the free breadsticks—we go for the fried lasagna. The restaurant's menu is a treasure trove of ideas, and when Lauren found this gem, we were immediately in love. Do not let the process frighten you: These are so much easier than they seem.

Cooking spray

10 lasagna noodles, cooked according to package instructions

1 (15-ounce) container ricotta

4 large eggs, divided

2 cloves garlic, minced

Kosher salt

Freshly ground black pepper

1 cup shredded mozzarella

½ cup all-purpose flour

2 cups Italian breadcrumbs

Vegetable oil, for frying

Marinara, warmed, for dipping

1. Grease a large baking sheet with cooking spray. Place cooked lasagna noodles in an even layer on top.

2. In a medium bowl, stir together ricotta, 1 egg, and garlic and season with salt and pepper. Spread on each lasagna noodle and sprinkle with mozzarella.

3. Fold each lasagna noodle three or four times to create a square. Freeze on prepared baking sheet until firm, 30 minutes.

4. When ready to cook, put flour, remaining 3 eggs, and breadcrumbs in three separate shallow bowls. Whisk eggs until beaten and season breadcrumbs with salt and pepper. Working in batches, dredge lasagna squares in flour, then dip in eggs, and finally toss in breadcrumbs to coat.

5. In a large deep-sided skillet over medium heat, heat 1½ inches oil until shimmering (about 350°F). Using tongs, add 3 or 4 lasagna squares and cook until golden, 2 to 3 minutes per side. Drain lasagna squares on a paper towel–lined wire rack. Repeat with remaining lasagna squares.

6. Serve with marinara.

TUSCAN TORTELLINI SOUP

TOTAL TIME: 40 MIN / SERVES 6

In August, when most people are starting to get excited
about pumpkin spice lattes, we're getting excited for fall soups.
This recipe is almost like a pasta stew; the tortellini soaks up
a lot of broth, and you'll want to drink what's left.

1 tablespoon extra-virgin
olive oil

1 medium yellow onion,
chopped

1 pound cooked chicken
sausage links, sliced
into ½-inch-thick
rounds

3 cloves garlic, minced

1 (28-ounce) can
crushed tomatoes

6 cups low-sodium
chicken broth

1 teaspoon crushed red
pepper flakes

Kosher salt

Freshly ground black
pepper

2 (9-ounce) packages
refrigerated cheese
tortellini

1 (15-ounce) can white
beans, drained

5 ounces baby spinach

Freshly grated
Parmesan, for serving

1. In a large pot over medium heat, heat oil. Add onion and cook, stirring, until soft, about 5 minutes. Add chicken sausage and cook until golden, about 4 minutes, then add garlic and cook until fragrant, 1 minute more. Stir in crushed tomatoes, broth, and red pepper flakes and season generously with salt and pepper.

2. Bring to a boil and add tortellini. Reduce heat to medium-low and simmer until tortellini is cooked and flavors start to meld, 18 to 20 minutes.

3. Stir in white beans and spinach and cook until spinach has wilted, 2 minutes more.

4. Serve with Parmesan.

CHICKEN ALFREDO ROLL-UPS

TOTAL TIME: 45 MIN / SERVES 4

When done right, Alfredo's the silent killer of pasta sauces; the jarred stuff will never beat homemade. These lasagna roll-ups are a comforting cheese coma you won't want to wake up from.

4 tablespoons butter

2 cloves garlic, minced

¼ cup all-purpose flour

2½ cups milk (preferably whole or 2%)

½ (8-ounce) block cream cheese, softened

½ cup freshly grated Parmesan

Juice of 1 lemon

1 tablespoon freshly chopped parsley

Kosher salt

Freshly ground black pepper

4 cups shredded rotisserie chicken

12 lasagna noodles, cooked according to package directions

1. Preheat oven to 350°F.

2. In a large skillet over medium heat, melt butter. Add garlic and cook until fragrant, 1 minute. Whisk in flour and cook 1 minute more. Pour in milk, whisking constantly, and bring mixture to a simmer. Stir in cream cheese and Parmesan and simmer until sauce thickens, 2 to 3 minutes. Add lemon juice and parsley and season with salt and pepper.

3. Spoon a thin layer of sauce onto bottom of a baking dish. Spread sauce onto each cooked noodle and top with chicken, then roll up noodle. Place roll-ups in baking dish, seam-side down, and spoon over remaining sauce.

4. Bake until chicken is warmed through, about 20 minutes.

WTF?

FRIED MAC & CHEESE

CHUCK AND BLADE / New York, NY

The version of mac & cheese that you'll find on the menu at Chuck and Blade barely resembles the version you ate as a kid. For starters, it's shaped into a ball. Second, it's deep-fried. And third, it's covered with super-thick cheese sauce. This place calls it—appropriately— the Bocce Ball, but this thing is no game. The cheesy center is made with Gruyère, fontina, and mozzarella, the same cheeses that are poured on top. The Bocce Ball has become one of the restaurant's most popular dishes. It turns heads whenever it's delivered to a table, and servers have never cleared a plate that hasn't been completely devoured.

4 WAYS TO USE RAMEN NOODLES

We couldn't have survived college without this staple,
and we couldn't live without it now.

1

ASIAN CHICKEN NOODLE SOUP

In a large pot, heat 1 tablespoon coconut oil. Add 1 chopped yellow onion, 2 chopped red bell peppers, and 1 thinly sliced carrot and cook, stirring, until soft. Add 2 minced cloves garlic, 1 tablespoon curry powder, and ½ teaspoon cayenne pepper and season with salt. Add 2 (15-ounce) cans coconut milk and 3 cups chicken broth and bring to a simmer. Add 2 cups shredded rotisserie chicken, ⅓ cup freshly chopped cilantro, and 1 packet ramen noodles and cook until noodles are al dente. Serve with lime.

2

BREAKFAST RAMEN

Cook 2 packets ramen noodles. In a nonstick skillet over medium heat, cook 6 slices chopped bacon until crispy. Add cooked ramen noodles and toss. Turn off heat. Whisk together 2 beaten large eggs and 1 cup shredded cheddar cheese and add to skillet, tossing until noodles are coated and cheese is melty. Garnish with green onions.

3

GARLIC-PARMESAN RAMEN

Cook 3 packets ramen noodles. In a large skillet over medium heat, melt 3 tablespoons butter. Cook 2 minced cloves garlic until fragrant, 1 minute, then add cooked ramen noodles and 1 cup freshly grated Parmesan. Toss to combine and garnish with freshly chopped parsley.

4

TRAVELING NOODLES

Cook 1 packet ramen noodles. Place ¼ vegetable bouillon cube, ¼ teaspoon freshly minced ginger, and ¼ cup shredded rotisserie chicken into each of four mason jars. Drizzle soy sauce and hot sauce into each jar, then divide cooked ramen evenly among each. Layer ¼ cup each baby spinach, matchstick carrots, and sliced green onions into each jar and refrigerate until ready to eat. When ready to eat, pour in boiling water. Let sit 3 minutes, then stir until combined.

ASIAN CHICKEN NOODLE SOUP

BOLOGNESE BAKED TORTELLINI

TOTAL TIME: 35 MIN / SERVES 6

When you want to make homemade sauce but don't have time to let it simmer for hours and hours, this shortcut Bolognese is the answer. What's even better: The sauce cooks the tortellini as it bakes, so you don't even have to dirty a pot.

2 tablespoons extra-virgin olive oil, plus more for baking dish

1 onion, chopped

3 cloves garlic, minced

1½ pounds ground beef

½ cup dry red wine, such as cabernet or merlot

2 tablespoons tomato paste

1 (28-ounce) can crushed tomatoes

1 teaspoon dried oregano

Kosher salt

Freshly ground black pepper

2 (9-ounce) packages refrigerated cheese tortellini

2 cups shredded mozzarella

2 tablespoons freshly grated Parmesan

Freshly sliced basil, for garnish

1. Preheat oven to 350°F and grease a large baking dish with oil.

2. In a large pot over medium heat, heat oil. Add onion and cook, stirring, until soft, 5 minutes. Add garlic and cook until fragrant, 1 minute. Add ground beef and cook, breaking up meat with a wooden spoon, until no longer pink, about 6 minutes. Drain fat.

3. Return beef mixture to skillet over medium heat and pour in wine, using a wooden spoon to scrape up any browned bits from bottom of pan. Cook until reduced by about half, then add tomato paste, crushed tomatoes, and oregano and season with salt and pepper. Bring mixture to a simmer and cook until slightly reduced, about 10 minutes.

4. Put tortellini in prepared baking dish. Pour over meat sauce and stir until coated. Top with mozzarella and Parmesan, then cover dish with foil.

5. Bake until cheese has melted and pasta is cooked through, 25 minutes.

6. Garnish with basil before serving.

CHAPTER EIGHT

TEX-MEX MADNESS

BEEF TACO BOATS

TOTAL TIME: 30 MIN / SERVES 4

Fact: Eating tacos out of a tortilla shaped like a boat is WAY more fun—you'll feel like you're out dining out even though you're not.

4 medium flour tortillas

Uncooked rice

1 tablespoon extra-virgin olive oil

1 onion, chopped

2 cloves garlic

1 pound ground beef

1 teaspoon chili powder

¼ teaspoon paprika

Kosher salt

Freshly ground black pepper

Shredded lettuce

Shredded cheddar cheese

Pico de gallo

Guacamole

Sour cream

1. Preheat oven to 350°F.

2. Shape a large piece of foil (smaller than the size of your tortillas) into a boat **A**. Place one tortilla inside foil boat so that the perimeter of tortilla comes up the sides **B**. Repeat to make 4 boats. Fill each boat with rice **C**.

3. Bake until lightly golden, about 15 minutes. Let cool in foil until ready to serve.

4. Meanwhile, in a large skillet over medium heat, heat oil. Add onion and cook, stirring, until soft, about 5 minutes. Add garlic and cook until fragrant, 1 minute more. Add ground beef, chili powder, and paprika and season with salt and pepper. Cook, breaking up meat with a wooden spoon, until beef is no longer pink, about 6 minutes. Drain fat.

5. Remove rice and foil from tortilla boats and fill each with ground beef. Top with lettuce, cheddar cheese, pico de gallo, guacamole, and sour cream.

WATCH & LEARN

A   B   C

CRUNCHWRAP SUPREME

TOTAL TIME: 45 MIN / SERVES 4

If you've ever been at a Taco Bell at 2 a.m., chances are you ordered a Crunchwrap, the chain's beloved drunk food. Ours is every bit as good as the real thing—believe it.

1 pound ground beef

1 teaspoon chili powder

½ teaspoon ground paprika

½ teaspoon ground cumin

Kosher salt

Freshly ground black pepper

8 large flour tortillas

½ cup nacho cheese sauce

4 tostada shells

1 cup sour cream

2 cups shredded lettuce

1 cup chopped tomatoes

1 cup shredded cheddar cheese

1 cup shredded Monterey jack cheese

1 tablespoon vegetable oil

1. In a large nonstick skillet over medium heat, combine ground beef and spices and season with salt and pepper. Cook, breaking up meat with a wooden spoon, until no longer pink, about 6 minutes. Drain fat and wipe skillet clean.

2. Stack 4 large flour tortillas and place a tostada shell in the center. Using a paring knife, trace around edges of shell to cut 4 smaller flour tortilla rounds.

3. Build Crunchwraps: Add a scoop of ground beef to the center of remaining 4 large flour tortillas, leaving a generous border for folding. Drizzle cheese sauce over each **Ⓐ**, then place a tostada shell on top. Spread sour cream over each shell, then top with lettuce, tomato, and cheeses. Place smaller flour tortilla cutouts on top **Ⓑ** and tightly fold edges of large tortilla toward the center, creating pleats **Ⓒ**. Quickly invert Crunchwraps so pleats are on the bottom and they stay together.

4. In the same skillet over medium heat, heat oil. Add Crunchwrap seam-side down and cook until tortilla is golden, 3 minutes per side **Ⓓ**. Repeat with remaining Crunchwraps.

WATCH & LEARN

Ⓐ　　　Ⓑ　　　Ⓒ　　　Ⓓ

MEXICAN CHICKEN PASTA

TOTAL TIME: 40 MIN / SERVES 4

All the best flavors of fajitas, only with spaghetti instead of tortillas. Don't try to understand.

12 ounces spaghetti

1 tablespoon extra-virgin olive oil

1 pound boneless, skinless chicken breasts, cut into 1-inch pieces

Kosher salt

Freshly ground black pepper

1 large onion, sliced into half moons

2 bell peppers, sliced

1 tablespoon chili powder

1 tablespoon ground cumin

2 teaspoons dried oregano

1 (15-ounce) can fire-roasted diced tomatoes

½ cup low-sodium chicken broth

¾ cup half-and-half

½ cup shredded cheddar cheese

½ cup shredded pepper jack cheese

Freshly chopped cilantro, for garnish

1. In a large pot of salted boiling water, cook spaghetti according to package directions until al dente. Drain.

2. Meanwhile, in a large skillet over medium-high heat, heat oil. Add chicken and season with salt and pepper. Cook, stirring occasionally, until golden, about 6 minutes, then add onion and bell peppers and cook, stirring, until soft, 5 to 7 minutes more. Add spices and stir until coated.

3. Stir in tomatoes, broth, and half-and-half and simmer until slightly reduced, about 3 minutes. Add cooked spaghetti and toss until coated, then remove from heat, add cheeses, and stir until melty and creamy. Season with salt and pepper.

4. Garnish with cilantro before serving.

SLOW-COOKER CARNITAS

TOTAL TIME: 4 HRS 20 MIN / SERVES 6

Our two food editors from California are constantly whining about how they can't find good carnitas in New York, so they made their own. They wanted the recipe to be a flavor bomb, but also easy (you will not be searing a huge pork shoulder). Homesick cooking at its best.

1 tablespoon ground cumin

1 tablespoon kosher salt

1 tablespoon chili powder

1 teaspoon dried oregano

1 teaspoon freshly ground black pepper

¼ teaspoon ground cinnamon

1 (2- to 3-pound) boneless pork shoulder

1 large onion, quartered

5 cloves garlic, smashed

1 cup lager beer

Juice of 3 limes

Tortillas, for serving

1. In a medium bowl, whisk together salt and spices. Rub mixture all over pork shoulder.

2. Place onion and garlic in slow cooker, then place pork shoulder on top and pour over lager and lime juice.

3. Cover and cook on high for 4 to 5 hours or low for 8 to 10, until pork is very tender.

4. Let rest 30 minutes, then use forks to shred pork, discarding fat. Return meat to cooking liquid in slow cooker and toss to coat.

5. Preheat broiler. Transfer shredded pork to a large baking sheet and broil until crispy, 5 minutes.

6. Serve in tortillas.

These make an amazing **BREAKFAST HASH** with crispy potatoes, eggs, and Monterey jack cheese.

TAMALE PIE

TOTAL TIME: 50 MIN / SERVES 8

If you're making tamale pie with cornbread on TOP, you're doing it wrong—it's the perfect crust. After it bakes, poke holes all over and pour over enchilada sauce. It seeps inside for an insane experience.

Cooking spray

1 box corn muffin mix (such as JIFFY)

1 large egg

½ cup sour cream

½ cup canned creamed corn

1 tablespoon extra-virgin olive oil

1 onion, chopped

1 teaspoon ground cumin

1 teaspoon chili powder

Kosher salt

Freshly ground black pepper

2 cloves garlic, minced

1 pound ground beef

1 cup canned black beans, drained and rinsed

⅓ cup red enchilada sauce

1 cup shredded cheddar cheese

1 cup shredded Monterey jack cheese

1. Preheat oven to 400°F. Grease a large oven-safe skillet with cooking spray.

2. In a large bowl, whisk together corn muffin mix, egg, sour cream, and creamed corn. Transfer to prepared skillet and bake until golden, 20 minutes. Let cool.

3. Meanwhile, in a large skillet over medium heat, heat oil. Add onion, cumin, and chili powder and season with salt and pepper. Cook until soft, 5 minutes. Add garlic and cook until fragrant, 1 minute more. Add ground beef and cook, breaking up meat with a wooden spoon, until no longer pink, about 6 minutes. Drain the fat, then stir in the black beans.

4. Poke entire surface of cornbread with a fork and pour over enchilada sauce. Add beef and top with cheeses.

5. Cover with foil and bake until cheese is melty, about 20 minutes. Switch oven to broil, remove foil, and broil until cheese turns golden, about 5 minutes.

LOADED NACHO SOUP

TOTAL TIME: 25 MIN / SERVES 6

When you're as obsessed with nachos as we are (see the proof on pages 52–53), you break the rules and turn soup into an over-the-top cheesy dinner. The crazier the toppings, the better: Tortilla chips, sour cream, salsa, and guac all work.

- 1 tablespoon extra-virgin olive oil
- 1 medium onion, chopped
- 2 cloves garlic, minced
- 1 tablespoon ground cumin
- 1 tablespoon chili powder
- ½ teaspoon cayenne pepper
- 1 (15-ounce) can fire-roasted diced tomatoes
- 1 (15-ounce) can corn kernels, drained
- 1 (15 ounce) can black beans, drained and rinsed
- 2 cups shredded rotisserie chicken
- 4 cups low-sodium chicken broth
- ¾ cup heavy cream
- 1 cup shredded pepper jack cheese
- ½ cup shredded cheddar cheese
- Sour cream, for serving
- Crushed tortilla chips, for serving
- Freshly chopped cilantro, for serving

1. In a large pot over medium heat, heat oil. Add onion and cook, stirring, until soft, about 5 minutes. Add garlic and spices and cook until fragrant, 1 minute.

2. Add tomatoes, corn, black beans, and chicken and stir until combined, then pour over broth.

3. Bring to a simmer and cook 15 minutes, then stir in heavy cream and cheeses and cook until cheese is melty.

4. Top soup with sour cream, tortilla chips, and cilantro before serving.

MONSTER BURRITO

TAQUERIA CANCÚN / San Francisco, CA

RESTAURANT OMG! PORN

Our creative director Nick told us that everyone in San Francisco knows exactly where to go for the best burrito: the Mission . . . specifically Taqueria Cancún. It's not super trendy or fancy, but the restaurant specializes in behemoth burritos each the size of a football. The options extend well beyond what you'd find at Chipotle, but if you only have room for one food coma–inducing dish, you've got to go for the meal that's made Taqueria Cancún a cult favorite: the *burrito mojado*, or "wet burrito." The entire thing's covered in enchilada sauce, then blanketed in shredded cheese. It's garnished with salsa verde, sour cream, and classic red salsa, forming stripes across the dish in a nod to the Mexican flag. Even on an empty stomach, it's hard to get through half before tapping out.

TEQUILA-LIME CHICKEN TACOS

TOTAL TIME: 45 MIN / SERVES 4

When we first made these we added three times the amount of tequila we should have (we like to freestyle, okay?!) and felt drunk almost immediately. The now tweaked recipe won't get you buzzed, but will make you MVP of Taco Tuesday.

½ cup tequila

Juice of 4 limes

2 cloves garlic, minced

2 jalapeños: 1 finely chopped and 1 sliced, divided

Freshy ground black pepper

Kosher salt

1 pound boneless, skinless chicken breasts

1 tablespoon vegetable oil

Corn tortillas, warmed, for serving

1 avocado, sliced

¼ head red cabbage, shredded

½ cup cotija cheese

Lime wedges, for serving

1. In a large baking dish, whisk together tequila, lime juice, garlic, and chopped jalapeño and season with salt and pepper. Add chicken and marinate in the fridge at least 20 minutes and up to 1 hour.

2. In a grill pan or skillet over medium-high heat, heat oil. Cook chicken until golden and no longer pink inside, about 8 minutes per side. Let rest 10 minutes before slicing.

3. Serve in tortillas with avocado, cabbage, sliced jalapeño, and cotija, and squeeze with lime.

Don't have a **SPRINGFORM PAN?** A standard cake or pie pan totally works here. You'll just need to serve your cake IN the pan.

QUESADILLA CAKE

TOTAL TIME: 45 MIN / SERVES 6

We know plenty of people who would way rather devour a slice of this on their birthday than actual cake. We don't blame them: Five layers of flour tortillas, seasoned ground beef, and melty cheese are what dreams are made of.

Cooking spray

1 tablespoon extra-virgin olive oil

1 large onion, chopped

2 cloves garlic, minced

1 teaspoon chili powder

1 teaspoon ground cumin

1 pound ground beef

2 tomatoes, chopped

2 tablespoons tomato paste

Kosher salt

Freshly ground black pepper

6 medium flour tortillas

1 cup shredded cheddar cheese

1 cup shredded Monterey jack cheese

TOPPINGS

Pico de gallo

Sour cream

Fresh cilantro

1. Preheat oven to 400°F and grease an 8- or 9-inch springform pan with cooking spray.

2. In a large skillet over medium heat, heat oil. Add onion and cook, stirring, until soft, about 5 minutes, then add garlic and spices and cook until fragrant, 1 minute. Add ground beef and cook, breaking up meat with a wooden spoon, until no longer pink, about 6 minutes. Drain fat.

3. Return beef mixture to skillet over medium heat and stir in tomatoes and tomato paste. Cook 2 minutes more, then season with salt and pepper.

4. Build cake: Place a tortilla on bottom of prepared springform pan. Top with a layer of beef mixture and a handful of both cheeses. Repeat for five layers total, ending with cheese.

5. Bake until cheese is melty and tortillas are warmed through, 20 minutes. Let cool in pan 5 minutes.

6. Garnish with desired toppings before slicing and serving.

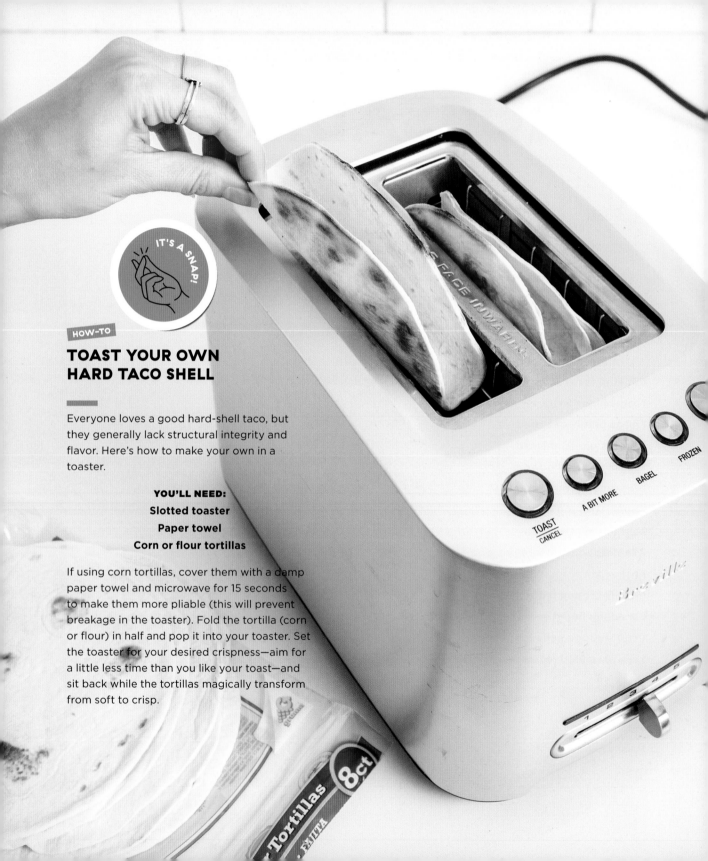

HOW-TO

TOAST YOUR OWN HARD TACO SHELL

Everyone loves a good hard-shell taco, but they generally lack structural integrity and flavor. Here's how to make your own in a toaster.

YOU'LL NEED:
Slotted toaster
Paper towel
Corn or flour tortillas

If using corn tortillas, cover them with a damp paper towel and microwave for 15 seconds to make them more pliable (this will prevent breakage in the toaster). Fold the tortilla (corn or flour) in half and pop it into your toaster. Set the toaster for your desired crispness—aim for a little less time than you like your toast—and sit back while the tortillas magically transform from soft to crisp.

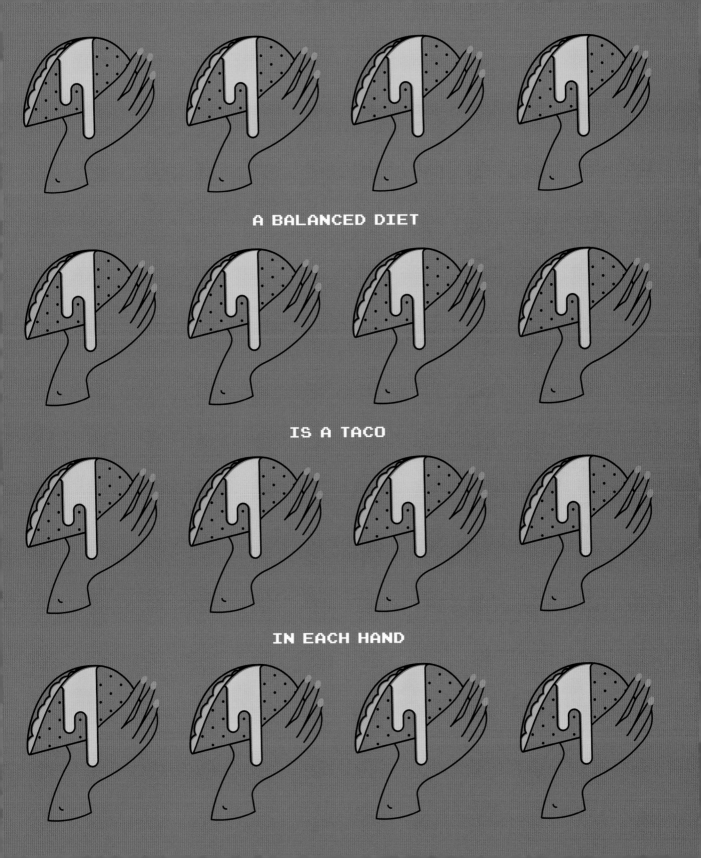

A BALANCED DIET

IS A TACO

IN EACH HAND

TEX-MEX MEATBALLS

TOTAL TIME: 30 MIN / SERVES 4

It's time to change up your meatball game, and these are irresistible. Case in point: When a skillet of them arrived to the Delish floor right after everyone had just finished a huge lunch, they were STILL gone in 20 seconds.

1½ pounds ground beef

2 cups shredded Mexican cheese blend, divided

½ cup panko breadcrumbs

2 tablespoons freshly chopped parsley, plus more for garnish

2 cloves garlic, minced

1 jalapeño, finely chopped

1 large egg

1 teaspoon ground cumin

Kosher salt

Freshly ground black pepper

1 tablespoon extra-virgin olive oil

½ large onion, chopped

1 (15-ounce) can crushed tomatoes

2 tablespoons chopped chipotle chiles in adobo sauce

1. In a medium bowl, combine ground beef, 1 cup of cheese, breadcrumbs, parsley, garlic, jalapeño, egg, and cumin and season with salt and pepper. Mix until combined, then form into meatballs.

2. In a large skillet over medium-high heat, heat oil. Add meatballs in a single layer and sear 2 minutes per side. Transfer to a plate.

3. Add onion to skillet and cook, stirring, until soft, 5 minutes. Stir in crushed tomatoes and chipotle in adobo and bring mixture to a boil. Reduce heat to medium-low and return meatballs to skillet. Cover and simmer until meatballs are cooked through, about 10 minutes.

4. Top with remaining 1 cup cheese, then cover with lid to let melt, about 2 minutes.

5. Garnish with parsley before serving.

These meatballs make a KILLER SUB: Throw them on a hero roll with extra sauce and melt some cheddar on top.

CHEESY MEXICAN CAULI RICE

TOTAL TIME: 20 MIN / SERVES 4

That moment when we drown our low-carb dread in enough cheddar and Monterey jack cheese to be like, "What's a diet?"

1 tablespoon extra-virgin olive oil, plus more if needed

1 medium onion, chopped

2 cloves garlic, minced

1 teaspoon dried oregano

½ teaspoon ground cumin

1 large head cauliflower, grated, or 4 cups riced cauliflower

Kosher salt

Freshly ground black pepper

1 tablespoon tomato paste

2 cups shredded rotisserie chicken

1 (15-ounce) can black beans, drained and rinsed

1 cup corn kernels (fresh, canned, or thawed frozen)

1 cup chopped tomatoes

2 jalapeños, thinly sliced

¼ cup freshly chopped cilantro

1 cup shredded cheddar cheese

1 cup shredded Monterey jack cheese

Lime wedges, for serving

1. In a large skillet over medium heat, heat oil. Add onion and cook until soft, 5 minutes. Add garlic, oregano, and cumin and cook until fragrant, 1 minute.

2. Put grated cauliflower in a clean dishtowel and twist to drain excess liquid.

3. Add a splash more oil to skillet if it seems dry, then add drained grated cauliflower and season with salt and pepper. Cook, stirring occasionally, until tender, 3 to 5 minutes, then add tomato paste and stir until combined. Stir in chicken, black beans, corn, tomatoes, jalapeños, and cilantro.

4. Top with cheeses and cover with lid to let melt, 2 minutes.

5. Serve with limes.

CHICKEN ENCHILADA SKILLET

TOTAL TIME: 1 HR 15 MIN / SERVES 6

This was one of Lauren's first recipes at Delish, and everyone FREAKED OUT when they tasted it. She makes her own enchilada sauce, and it's just that good: rich, smoky, not too spicy. She eats these leftovers topped with a fried egg because she's an evil genius.

1 tablespoon extra-virgin olive oil

½ onion, finely chopped

2 cloves garlic, minced

2 tablespoons all-purpose flour

2 tablespoons tomato paste

1½ cups low-sodium chicken broth

1 (15-ounce) can tomato sauce

2 tablespoons chili powder

1 teaspoon ground cumin

¼ teaspoon paprika

Pinch cayenne pepper

Kosher salt

Freshly ground black pepper

3 cups shredded rotisserie chicken

15 to 20 corn tortillas

1½ cups shredded cheddar cheese

1½ cups shredded Monterey jack cheese

TOPPINGS
Sliced avocado

Sliced green onions

Sour cream

Hot sauce

1. Preheat oven to 375°F.

2. In a large skillet over medium heat, heat oil. Add onion and cook, stirring, until soft, about 5 minutes. Add garlic and cook until fragrant, 1 minute. Whisk in flour and cook 1 minute more. Add tomato paste and stir to combine.

3. Add broth, tomato sauce, and spices and season with salt and pepper. Bring mixture to a boil, then reduce heat to low and simmer 10 to 15 minutes. Stir in chicken.

4. Spread thin layer of enchilada sauce over bottom of a large oven-safe skillet. Place a single layer of tortillas on top, then top with a third each of the chicken mixture, cheeses, and enchilada sauce. Repeat layering process twice more, ending with cheese.

5. Cover with foil and bake until cheese is melty, 25 to 30 minutes. Let rest in skillet at least 10 minutes.

6. Garnish with desired toppings before slicing and serving.

QUESADILLA BURGER

TOTAL TIME: 30 MIN / SERVES 4

Does the world really need a quesadilla burger? No. But does the world really WANT a quesadilla burger? Once you take a bite of this baby, there won't be any question.

1 pound ground beef

1 clove garlic, minced

1 jalapeño, minced

1 teaspoon chili powder

Kosher salt

Freshly ground black pepper

5 tablespoons vegetable oil, divided

8 small flour tortillas

1½ cups shredded cheddar cheese

1½ cups shredded Monterey jack cheese

1½ cups shredded lettuce

1 cup pico de gallo

½ cup sour cream, for drizzling

1. In a large bowl, combine ground beef, garlic, jalapeño, and chili powder and season with salt and pepper. Mix until just combined, then shape mixture into 4 thin patties.

2. In a large skillet over medium-high heat, heat 1 tablespoon of oil. Cook patties to your desired doneness, about 4 minutes per side for medium. Transfer to a plate and wipe skillet clean.

3. Heat 1 tablespoon oil over medium heat. Add a flour tortilla and top with a small handful each of cheeses and lettuce.

4. Place a cooked burger on top, then top with more cheese, and ¼ cup pico de gallo and a drizzle of sour cream. Top with a tortilla and cook until golden, about 2 minutes.

5. Flip quesadilla and cook 2 minutes more. Repeat with remaining ingredients to make 4 quesadilla burgers.

DELISH GOES TO . . .
THE ULTIMATE TACO BELL

It's only fitting that Taco Bell's largest fast-food joint is right in the heart of Sin City: It's a complete assault on your senses. The typical purple, plastic décor is replaced with a modern industrial vibe—think: exposed brick and white neon lights everywhere— and there's an entire wall of frozen drinks hypnotically spinning every flavor of Baja Blast you can imagine. Which you can order spiked, because this is Vegas. You'll find menu items you won't get anywhere else, like cheesy bacon jalapeño dippers and smothered potato nachos. As if that weren't enough, the place has its own gift shop (featuring taco hats and bikinis, natch), a DJ booth, and a chapel, so you can order a wedding just as casually as you do a Crunchwrap. Taco 'bout a good time.

CHAPTER NINE

GOOD FOR YOU!

You're trying to eat healthier. Respect.

TACO TOMATOES

TOTAL TIME: 25 MIN / SERVES 4

We might sound dorky, but some Delish recipes truly take our breath away, either because they look stunning, they're totally surprising, or they're so so delicious. When one recipe hits all three, you know it's a keeper. These tomatoes are a genius low-carb hack.

1 tablespoon extra-virgin olive oil

1 medium onion, chopped

¾ pound ground beef

1 (1-ounce) packet taco seasoning

4 large, ripe beefsteak tomatoes

½ cup shredded Mexican cheese blend

½ cup shredded iceberg lettuce

¼ cup sour cream

1. In a large skillet over medium heat, heat oil. Add onion and cook, stirring, until soft, 5 minutes. Add ground beef and taco seasoning. Cook, breaking up meat with a wooden spoon, until no longer pink, 8 minutes. Drain fat.

2. Flip over tomatoes so they're stem-side down and slice to make 6 wedges, being careful not to cut all the way through. Carefully spread open wedges.

3. Divide taco meat among tomatoes, then top each with cheese, lettuce, and sour cream before serving.

Stuff these **LASAGNA-STYLE:** Top with a little ricotta, mozzarella, and basil and bake for 15 minutes at 350°F.

BUDDHA BOWLS

TOTAL TIME: 40 MIN / SERVES 4

TBH, when we first came across the Buddha bowl trend on Pinterest, we weren't sure how our audience was going to react. We found the perfect balance here between healthy and fun: If we could eat the peanut butter–sesame dressing every day, we would.

1 large sweet potato, peeled and cut into ½-inch cubes

1 large red onion, diced

3 tablespoons extra-virgin olive oil, divided

Kosher salt

Freshly ground black pepper

1 pound boneless, skinless chicken breasts

½ teaspoon garlic powder

½ teaspoon ground ginger

1 small clove garlic, minced

2 tablespoons creamy peanut butter

Juice of 1 lime

1 tablespoon low-sodium soy sauce

1 tablespoon honey

1 tablespoon toasted sesame oil

4 cups cooked brown rice

1 avocado, thinly sliced

2 cups baby spinach

Freshly chopped cilantro, for garnish

Toasted sesame seeds, for garnish

1. Preheat oven to 425°F.

2. On a large baking sheet, toss sweet potatoes and onion with 1 tablespoon of olive oil and season with salt and pepper. Bake until tender, 20 to 25 minutes.

3. Meanwhile, in a large skillet over medium-high heat, heat 1 tablespoon of olive oil. Season chicken with garlic powder, ginger, salt, and pepper. Cook until golden and no longer pink inside, 8 minutes per side. Let rest 10 minutes, then slice.

4. In a small bowl, whisk together garlic, peanut butter, lime juice, soy sauce, and honey. Whisk in sesame oil and remaining 1 tablespoon olive oil until smooth.

5. Divide rice among four bowls and top each with sweet potato mixture, chicken, avocado, and baby spinach, dividing them evenly. Sprinkle with cilantro and sesame seeds and drizzle with dressing before serving.

CHICKEN FRIED CAULIFLOWER

TOTAL TIME: 35 MIN / SERVES 4

We hear you: "HOW IS THIS EVEN HEALTHY?" But once you try this insanity—crispy, tender, and caramelized —you won't even care.

1 large head cauliflower, sliced into 1-inch-thick steaks

1 cup all-purpose flour

1 teaspoon garlic powder

½ teaspoon paprika

Kosher salt

3 large eggs

Vegetable oil, for frying

Hot Honey

1. Place cauliflower steaks in a large deep-sided skillet and add enough water to come halfway up sides of cauliflower. Bring to a simmer over medium heat, cover, and steam until fork-tender, 4 to 5 minutes. Drain and let cool completely.

2. Meanwhile, in a shallow bowl, whisk together flour, garlic powder, and paprika and season with salt. In another shallow bowl, lightly beat eggs. Toss cooled cauliflower in flour mixture, then dip in eggs, then return to flour mixture and toss again until completely coated.

3. In a skillet over medium-high heat, heat 1 inch of oil until it starts to bubble and looks shimmery. Carefully add cauliflower and fry until deeply golden, 2 minutes per side. Drain on a paper towel–lined plate.

4. Serve with Hot Honey.

HOT HONEY

Mix together ½ cup HONEY and 1 teaspoon HOT SAUCE. Put on everything.

BANG BANG BRUSSELS SPROUTS

TOTAL TIME: 50 MIN / SERVES 4

Brussels have come such a long way since their days as a boiled, tasteless sidekick. We'd choose eating a whole sheet pan of these over a salad any day. The Bang Bang Sauce is basically just next-level Sriracha.

3 tablespoons extra-virgin olive oil

2 tablespoons sweet chili sauce

1 tablespoon Sriracha

Juice of 1 lime

3 cloves garlic, minced

2 pounds Brussels sprouts, trimmed and halved (quartered if large)

Kosher salt

Freshly ground black pepper

1. Preheat oven to 425°F.

2. In a small bowl, whisk together oil, sweet chili sauce, Sriracha, lime juice, and garlic.

3. On a large baking sheet, toss Brussels sprouts in sauce until fully coated and season generously with salt and pepper.

4. Roast until Brussels are slightly charred and tender, 30 to 35 minutes.

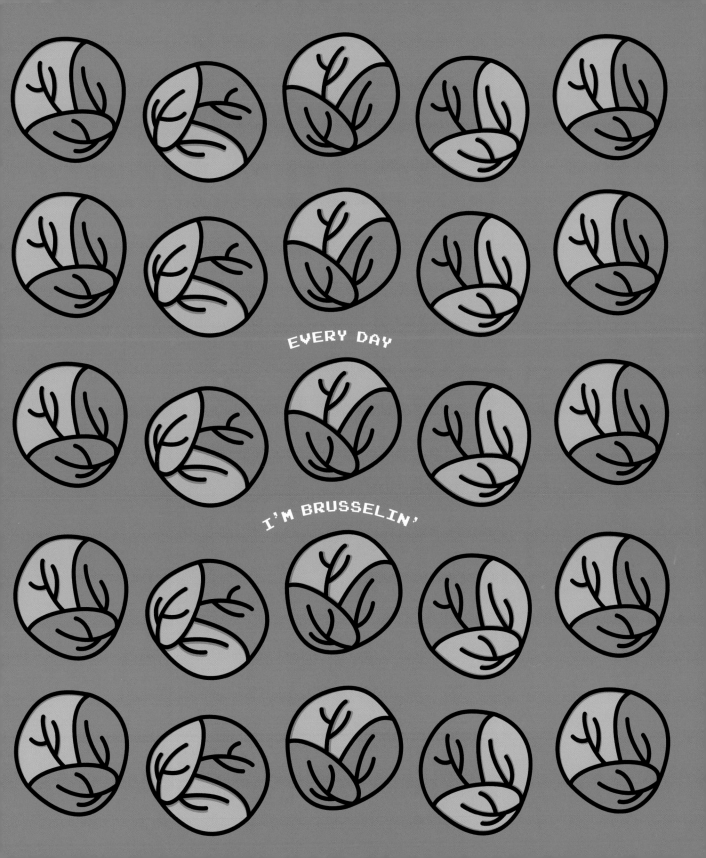

ZUCCHINI ENCHILADAS

TOTAL TIME: 40 MIN / SERVES 4

We've turned this squash into almost everything in the Delish kitchen: low-carb ravioli, taco shells, grilled cheese. Fill these with whatever enchilada filling you want (see page 236 for our perfect sauce) and get rolling.

1 tablespoon extra-virgin olive oil

1 large onion, chopped

2 cloves garlic, minced

2 teaspoons ground cumin

2 teaspoons chili powder

Kosher salt

3 cups shredded rotisserie chicken

1⅓ cups red enchilada sauce, divided

4 large zucchini, halved lengthwise

1 cup shredded Monterey jack cheese

1 cup shredded cheddar cheese

Sour cream, for drizzling

Fresh cilantro, for garnish

1. Preheat oven to 350°F.

2. In a large skillet over medium heat, heat oil. Add onion and cook, stirring, until soft, 5 minutes. Add garlic, cumin, and chili powder and season with salt. Cook until fragrant, about 1 minute. Add chicken and 1 cup of enchilada sauce and stir until coated.

3. On a cutting board, use a Y-shaped vegetable peeler to peel thin slices of zucchini. Lay out 3 slices, slightly overlapping, and top with a spoonful of chicken mixture. Roll up and transfer to a baking dish. Repeat with remaining zucchini and chicken mixture.

4. Spoon remaining ⅓ cup enchilada sauce over zucchini enchiladas and top with both cheeses.

5. Bake until cheese is melty and enchiladas are warmed through, 20 minutes.

6. Top with sour cream and cilantro before serving.

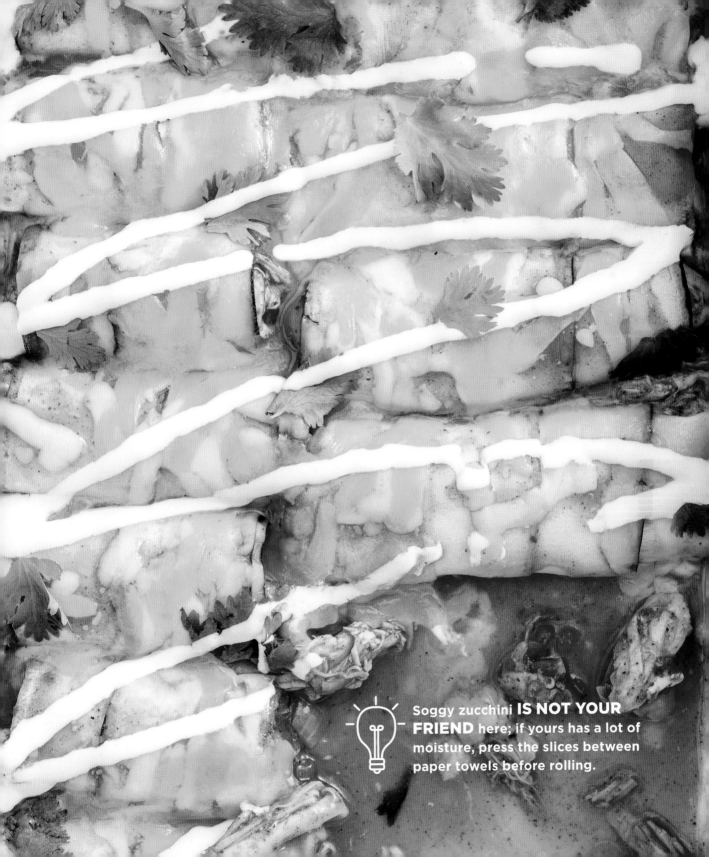

Soggy zucchini **IS NOT YOUR FRIEND** here; if yours has a lot of moisture, press the slices between paper towels before rolling.

LET'S GET STUFFED!

When lunch seems like the pits, it's time to pull out one of these brilliant stuffed avocados.

CAPRESE

+ CHERRY TOMATOES
+ FRESH MOZZARELLA
+ ITALIAN SEASONING
+ OIL AND VINEGAR
+ BASIL

SHRIMP SALAD

+ SAUTÉED SHRIMP
+ CHERRY TOMATOES
+ CORN
+ GREEK YOGURT
+ LEMON JUICE
+ BASIL

TEX-MEX

+ COOKED QUINOA
+ BLACK BEANS
+ RED BELL PEPPER
+ CORN
+ GREEN ONIONS
+ LIME JUICE

BLT

+ CHERRY TOMATOES
+ ROMAINE
+ CRUMBLED BACON
+ TOASTED BREAD
+ MAYO

CHICKEN SALAD

+ SHREDDED CHICKEN
+ RED ONION
+ MAYO
+ DIJON MUSTARD
+ GREEN ONIONS

OUTBACK'S SECRET SAUCE

In a medium bowl, whisk together ⅔ cup **MAYONNAISE**, 2 tablespoons **KETCHUP**, 1 teaspoon prepared **HORSERADISH**, ½ teaspoon **PAPRIKA**, ½ teaspoon **GARLIC POWDER**, and ¼ teaspoon **DRIED OREGANO**. Season with **SALT**.

BAKED BLOOMIN' ONION

TOTAL TIME: 35 MIN / SERVES 4

Everyone knows the Outback's version of this bad boy—but the idea of making a legit deep-fried version at home gives us hives. Ours is sliced and breaded, but then it's baked—and the resulting crispy "petals" are unreal, especially when dunked in our take on the chain's signature "bloom sauce."

1 large yellow onion

3 large eggs

1 cup breadcrumbs

2 teaspoons paprika

1 teaspoon garlic powder

1 teaspoon onion powder

Kosher salt

Outback's Secret Sauce

1. Preheat oven to 400°F and line a large baking sheet with parchment paper.

2. Slice off onion stem and set onion on flat side. Cut ½ inch from the root down, into 12 to 16 sections, being careful not to cut all the way through. Flip over and gently pull out sections of onion to separate petals.

3. In a shallow bowl, whisk together eggs and ¼ cup water. In another shallow bowl, whisk together breadcrumbs and spices and season with salt. Dip onion into egg wash, then dredge in breadcrumb mixture, using a spoon to fully coat.

4. Set onion on prepared baking sheet and bake until golden and tender, 18 to 20 minutes. Serve with Outback's Secret Sauce.

FYI: When perfecting his Bloomin' Onion recipe, the Outback Steakhouse founder worked with an **"ONION-OLOGIST"** (yup, that's a thing) at Texas A&M, who helped him create the perfect variety of onion for keeping its flower-like shape when it comes out of the fryer.

PARMESAN GARLIC CARROT FRIES

TOTAL TIME: 35 MIN / SERVES 4

How do you make carrots cool? Turn them into a version of ballpark garlic fries. They're light, crisp, and don't require a nap.

2 pounds carrots, peeled, halved, and sliced into thin matchsticks

2 tablespoons extra-virgin olive oil

¼ teaspoon paprika

Kosher salt

Freshly ground black pepper

3 cloves garlic, minced

¼ cup freshly grated Parmesan

Freshly chopped or dried parsley, for garnish

1. Preheat oven to 425°F.

2. Divide carrots between two large baking sheets and toss with oil and paprika. Season with salt and pepper and spread in an even layer. (This ensures they crisp up!)

3. Bake for 10 minutes, then toss carrots with garlic. Continue baking until tender and golden, 10 minutes more. Sprinkle with Parmesan and parsley before serving.

> We were making cookie fries in the kitchen, and we thought it would be fun if we served them in French fry containers. But, no joke, you can only buy these damn things in packs of, like, a thousand. Two years later, we still have eight hundred left. If you need any, call us. **—JO**

OVEN-FRIED PICKLES

TOTAL TIME: 25 MIN / SERVES 6

If you have to order fried pickles whenever you spot them on a menu—we particularly love the ones at Buffalo Wild Wings—you know they're worth every battered bite. But we wanted to see if we could bake up a healthier version. We did, and they're amazing.

1 cup panko breadcrumbs

¼ cup freshly chopped dill

2 tablespoons melted butter

½ teaspoon garlic powder

¼ teaspoon cayenne pepper

Kosher salt

Freshly ground black pepper

½ cup all-purpose flour

2 large eggs

1 cup pickle slices, patted dry with paper towels

Ranch dressing, for dipping

1. Preheat oven to 450°F and line a large baking sheet with parchment paper.

2. In a shallow bowl, stir together breadcrumbs, dill, melted butter, garlic powder, and cayenne and season with salt and pepper. Put flour in another shallow bowl. In a third bowl, beat eggs.

3. Working in batches, toss pickles in flour until lightly coated, then dip in eggs, then toss in panko mixture until fully coated.

4. Place pickles on prepared baking sheet and bake until golden and crispy, about 15 minutes.

5. Serve with ranch.

 Want to make these GLUTEN-FREE? Sub breadcrumbs for very finely chopped almonds.

BLT SUSHI

A peek inside our sick minds: When a recipe brainstorm starts with "What about a BLT rolled up inside bacon?!" BLT Sushi is born. You essentially make a giant bacon weave (see page 97), roll it up with lettuce, avocado, and tomato, slice, and stuff your face.

10 slices bacon

2 tablespoons mayonnaise

1 cup chopped tomatoes

½ avocado, diced

1 cup shredded romaine lettuce

Kosher salt

Freshly ground black pepper

1. Preheat oven to 400°F and place a wire rack over a large baking sheet.

2. Place 5 slices bacon side by side. Lift one end of every other bacon slice and place another bacon slice on top of the lifted pieces. Lay slices back. Next, lift opposite bacon slices back and place a bacon slice on top. Lay slices back down. Repeat weaving process until you have a bacon weave of 5 strips by 5 strips. Set bacon weave on prepared baking sheet.

3. Bake until bacon is cooked but still pliable, 20 minutes.

4. Pat bacon weave with paper towels to drain fat and transfer to a piece of plastic wrap (it helps with rolling!) **A**.

5. Spread mayo on top of bacon weave in a thin layer, then top bottom third of bacon weave with tomatoes and avocado. Sprinkle romaine all over and season with salt and pepper.

6. Starting from the bottom, tightly roll **B**,**C**, then slice crosswise into "sushi rolls" **D**.

— WATCH & LEARN —

A   **B**   **C**   **D**

DEATH BY CHOCOLATE
ZUCCHINI BREAD

DELISH FAVE

TOTAL TIME: 1 HR 5 MIN / SERVES 6

To be totally fair, zucchini bread is one of those halfway-healthy recipes that barely makes the cut. But it's got green in it—and that's good enough for us. This recipe is deeply chocolatey but also delightfully light—so you can eat an entire loaf while watching *Game of Thrones* and not totally lose your self-respect.

½ **cup (1 stick) melted butter, plus more for pan**

½ **cup unsweetened cocoa powder, plus more for pan**

1¼ **cups all-purpose flour**

1 **teaspoon baking soda**

1 **teaspoon ground cinnamon**

¼ **teaspoon kosher salt**

1 **cup sugar**

1 **large egg**

1 **large egg yolk**

1 **teaspoon pure vanilla extract**

2 **cups grated zucchini (from 1 large or 3 small)**

⅔ **cup semisweet chocolate chips**

Flaky sea salt

1. Preheat oven to 350°F. Butter a 9x5-inch loaf pan and dust with cocoa powder, tapping out any excess.

2. In a large bowl, whisk together flour, cocoa powder, baking soda, cinnamon, and salt.

3. In another large bowl, stir together sugar, egg, and egg yolk until smooth, 1 minute. Add melted butter and vanilla and mix until smooth, then fold in zucchini. Gradually add flour mixture, then fold in chocolate chips. Transfer batter to prepared pan.

4. Bake until a toothpick inserted into center comes out clean, 50 minutes.

5. Let bread cool in pan 10 minutes, then invert onto a wire rack to cool completely.

6. Sprinkle with flaky sea salt, slice, and serve.

CHICKEN
PARM
STUFFED
PEPPERS

4 WAYS TO MAKE STUFFED PEPPERS

Your mom's boring recipe is nowhere in sight.

1

CHICKEN PARM

In a large bowl, combine 2 cups shredded mozzarella, ½ cup grated Parmesan, 2 minced cloves garlic, and 1½ cups marinara and season with salt and pepper. Fold in 12 ounces chopped cooked breaded chicken, then spoon mixture into 4 halved bell peppers and sprinkle with 1 cup shredded mozzarella. Bake at 400°F until peppers are crisp-tender, 30 minutes.

2

LASAGNA

In a large skillet over medium heat, heat 1 tablespoon olive oil. Add ½ chopped onion and cook 5 minutes. Add ½ pound ground beef, and season with salt and pepper. Cook until no longer pink, 8 minutes. Stir in 1 (14.5-ounce) can tomato sauce and 1 teaspoon Italian seasoning. Let sauce thicken, 5 minutes. In a small bowl, stir ¾ cup ricotta, 1 large egg, and 2 tablespoons grated Parmesan and season with salt and pepper. Spoon meat sauce into 4 halved bell peppers and top with ricotta mixture, more meat sauce, and 1 cup shredded mozzarella. Bake at 400°F until crisp-tender, 30 minutes.

3

CHEESESTEAK

Place 4 halved bell peppers in a large baking dish and bake at 400°F until crisp-tender, 20 minutes. In a large skillet over medium-high heat, heat 1 tablespoon vegetable oil. Add 1½ pounds sliced sirloin steak and cook 1 minute per side; set aside. Add 1 sliced large onion and 16 ounces sliced mushrooms to skillet and season with salt and pepper. Cook 5 minutes, then stir in steak. Add 8 slices provolone cheese to bottom of peppers and top with steak mixture and 8 more slices provolone cheese and bake until melty.

4

RAGIN' CAJUN

In a large skillet over medium heat, heat 1 tablespoon olive oil. Add ½ chopped onion and cook about 5 minutes. Add 2 minced cloves garlic and cook 1 minute. Stir in 1 pound chopped andouille sausage, 1 cup corn, 1 cup chopped tomatoes, 2 tablespoons tomato paste, and 1 tablespoon Cajun seasoning and season with salt and pepper. Stir in 2 cups cooked rice and 1 cup shredded Monterey jack cheese. Spoon filling into 4 halved bell peppers and sprinkle with more cheese. Bake at 400°F until crisp-tender, 30 minutes.

BBQ CHICKEN TWICE-BAKED POTATOES

TOTAL TIME: 1 HR 30 MIN / SERVES 4

So many incredible things going on here: sweet potatoes, smoky cheese, spicy jalapeño, and tangy barbecue sauce. If you can find time to bake the sweet potatoes ahead of time, all you need is 20 minutes once you get home from work.

4 medium sweet potatoes

1 tablespoon extra-virgin olive oil

Kosher salt

Freshly ground black pepper

2 cups shredded rotisserie chicken

½ cup barbecue sauce, plus more for serving

2 cloves garlic, minced

½ small red onion, thinly sliced into quarter moons

1 small jalapeño, thinly sliced

1 cup shredded smoked Gouda

1. Preheat oven to 375°F.

2. Place sweet potatoes on a large baking sheet. Toss with oil and season with salt and pepper.

3. Bake until tender, about 1 hour, depending on size. Let cool slightly, then, using a paring knife, slice along top of each sweet potato and push in both ends to create a well.

4. In a medium bowl, toss chicken with barbecue sauce and garlic. Stuff into sweet potatoes, then top with red onion, jalapeño, and Gouda. Return to oven and bake until cheese is melty and chicken is warmed through, about 15 minutes more.

5. Drizzle with barbecue sauce before serving.

JALAPEÑO POPPER CRISPS

TOTAL TIME: 25 MIN / SERVES 8

These are our version of *frico*, the Parmesan crisps that fancy restaurants serve on salads—but they're also the only thing that will satisfy our very serious potato chip craving. Best part: They are almost too easy . . . just mounds of cheese, jalapeño, and bacon.

4 slices bacon

1 cup finely shredded Parmesan

½ cup shredded cheddar cheese (preferably aged)

1 jalapeño, sliced thinly

Freshly ground black pepper

1. Preheat oven to 375°F.

2. In a large nonstick skillet over medium heat, cook bacon until crispy, 8 minutes. Drain on a paper towel-lined plate, then chop.

3. Spoon about 1 tablespoon of Parmesan into a small mound on a large baking sheet and top with about ½ tablespoon of cheddar cheese. Carefully pat down cheeses and top with a jalapeño slice. Sprinkle with bacon and season with pepper. Repeat with remaining ingredients.

4. Bake until crispy and golden, about 12 minutes.

5. Let cool slightly on pan before serving.

STUFFED EGGPLANT PARM

TOTAL TIME: 1 HR 10 MIN / SERVES 4

We die for eggplant Parm when eggplants are in season, but the number of steps involved (Breading! Frying! Layering! Napping!) is such a turn-off. These boats are a perfect workaround: Scoop out the eggplant and sauté with tomatoes, then stuff with mozz and bake.

1½ cups marinara, divided

2 medium eggplants, halved

1 tablespoon extra-virgin olive oil

1 medium onion, chopped

1 teaspoon dried oregano

Kosher salt

Freshly ground black pepper

2 cloves garlic, minced

1 cup chopped tomatoes

1 large egg, lightly beaten

2½ cups shredded mozzarella, divided

¼ cup freshly grated Parmesan

2 tablespoons Italian breadcrumbs

Freshly sliced basil, for garnish

1. Preheat oven to 350°F.

2. Spread 1 cup of marinara over the bottom of a 9x13-inch baking dish. Using a spoon, hollow out eggplants, leaving about a ½-inch-thick border around skin to create a boat; transfer to baking dish. Roughly chop scooped-out eggplant flesh.

3. In a large skillet over medium heat, heat oil. Add onion and cook until soft, 5 minutes. Stir in chopped eggplant and season with oregano, salt, and pepper. Cook, stirring often, until golden and tender, 3 to 4 minutes. Add garlic and cook until fragrant, 1 minute.

4. Transfer mixture to a bowl and add tomatoes, egg, 1½ cups of mozzarella, and remaining ½ cup marinara. Mix until just combined, then scoop into eggplant boats. Top with remaining 1 cup mozzarella, Parmesan, and breadcrumbs.

5. Bake until eggplants are tender and cheese is golden, about 50 minutes.

6. Garnish with basil before serving.

CHAPTER TEN

BRUNCH TIME

Now serving all day.

BISCUITS & GRAVY PULL-APART SLIDERS

TOTAL TIME: 30 MIN / SERVES 8

We have an abnormal obsession with sausage gravy—we eat it straight with a spoon any time it's around. (When we shot these sliders, we couldn't help but dip bagel chips in the leftover gravy as a snack. Send help.) Makinze says the secret is in the freshly cracked black pepper: Season with twice as much as you think you should . . . and then add a little more. She's from Oklahoma, so she knows these things.

1 (16-ounce) can refrigerated biscuits

1 tablespoon melted butter

Freshly ground black pepper

1 pound Italian sausage (sweet or spicy), casings removed

¼ cup all-purpose flour

2¼ cups milk (preferably whole or 2%)

Kosher salt

Pinch cayenne pepper

1½ cups shredded cheddar cheese

Freshly chopped chives, for garnish

1. Preheat oven to 350°F and line a large baking sheet with parchment paper.

2. Place biscuits, touching, on prepared baking sheet in two rows of four. Brush with melted butter and season generously with pepper.

3. Bake until golden, about 18 minutes.

4. In a large skillet over medium heat, cook sausage, breaking up with a wooden spoon, until browned and no longer pink, 6 to 8 minutes. Sprinkle with flour and cook until completely absorbed, 1 minute. Pour over milk and bring mixture to a boil over high heat. Reduce heat to low and simmer, stirring occasionally, until thickened and slightly reduced, about 5 minutes. Remove from heat and season with salt, pepper, and cayenne.

5. Using a serrated knife, halve biscuits, trying to keep them connected as two sheets. Top bottom halves with sausage gravy, cheddar cheese, and biscuit tops.

6. Bake until cheese has melted, about 10 minutes more.

7. Sprinkle with chives before serving.

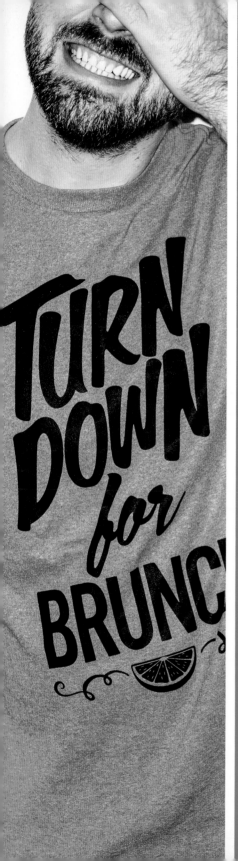

BREAKFAST PIZZA

TOTAL TIME: 50 MIN / SERVES 2

We kept seeing breakfast pizzas on brunch menus, but they all used a regular dough as the crust. That wasn't gonna cut it—we turned to our favorite breakfast ingredient: shredded hash browns. Each bite of crispy potatoes, savory bacon, and runny yolks will make you so happy you didn't just make another scramble.

Cooking spray

1 pound frozen shredded hash browns, thawed

6 large eggs, divided

2 cups shredded cheddar cheese, divided

Kosher salt

Freshly ground black pepper

6 slices bacon

Freshly chopped chives, for garnish

1. Preheat oven to 400°F and grease a large baking sheet with cooking spray.

2. In a large bowl, stir together hash browns, 2 eggs, and ½ cup of cheddar cheese and season with salt and pepper.

3. Transfer hash brown mixture to prepared baking sheet and, using your hands, pat into a circular crust. Bake until golden, 20 minutes.

4. In a large nonstick skillet over medium heat, cook bacon until crispy, 8 minutes. Drain on a paper towel-lined plate, then chop.

5. Top baked crust with remaining 1½ cups cheddar cheese and crack remaining 4 eggs on top. Scatter bacon over everything and season with salt and pepper.

6. Bake until egg whites are set but yolks are still slightly runny, 15 minutes. (If you prefer a less runny yolk, bake 18 to 20 minutes.)

7. Garnish with chives and slice.

GRILLED CHEESE
BLOODY MARYS

Basically the R-rated version of grilled cheese and tomato soup.
Your friends won't believe how genius you are.

2 cups tomato juice

8 ounces vodka

2 tablespoons Worcestershire sauce

1 tablespoon prepared horseradish

2 teaspoons hot sauce

Juice of ½ lemon

Freshly ground black pepper

4 slices bacon

2 tablespoons butter

4 slices white bread

4 slices cheddar cheese

Old Bay seasoning, for rimming glasses

Ice

4 pickle spears

1. In a large pitcher, stir together tomato juice, vodka, Worcestershire, horseradish, hot sauce, and lemon juice and season generously with pepper.

2. In a large nonstick skillet over medium heat, cook bacon until crispy, 8 minutes. Drain on a paper towel-lined plate. Wipe skillet clean.

3. Assemble sandwiches: Spread butter onto one side of each slice of bread. Place 2 slices cheddar cheese onto unbuttered side of two slices of bread, then top with remaining bread slices, buttered-side up.

4. In the same skillet over medium heat, cook sandwiches until bread is golden and cheese is melty, 4 to 5 minutes per side. Remove from skillet and cut each into four triangles.

5. Rim four glasses with a lemon wedge and dip in Old Bay.

6. Add ice to glasses and pour over Bloody Mary mixture. Garnish with grilled cheese, bacon, and a pickle.

BLOODY MARY BOMBS

TOTAL TIME: 2 HRS 5 MIN / MAKES 16

Part appetizer, part booze, with a bunch of bacon. These bombs are way more fun to serve friends than actual Bloody Marys: Cherry tomatoes and celery pieces soak in a doctored vodka and then get skewered with bacon and pickles. Don't throw too many back at once—they mean biz.

1 cup vodka

2 tablespoons Worcestershire sauce

2 teaspoons hot sauce

½ teaspoon lemon pepper

1 pint cherry tomatoes

2 stalks celery, chopped into ½-inch pieces

16 slices bacon

16 baby dill pickles or cornichons

1. In a large bowl, whisk together vodka, Worcestershire, hot sauce, and lemon pepper.

2. Add tomatoes and celery and let soak in refrigerator at least 2 hours and up to overnight.

3. In a large nonstick skillet over medium heat, cook bacon until crispy, but still pliable, 6 minutes. Drain on a paper towel-lined plate, then halve.

4. On each appetizer skewer, skewer 2 bacon halves, soaked tomatoes and celery, and a pickle.

HOW-TO

IT'S A SNAP!

THE MOST EGGSELLENT WAY TO SCRAMBLE

Rather than continue to fight your skillet every Sunday morning, there's a stupid-easy new hack for making scrambled eggs—and it's literally impossible to screw them up. All you need is a baking sheet. Beat your eggs as per usual in a large bowl, pour them on a greased baking sheet, then bake at 350°F until the eggs are set, about 12 minutes. You can sprinkle veggies, meat, and/or cheese on top before you bake them, or just leave your eggs au natural. You'll get perfectly set, light, and fluffy eggs every time.

BIRTHDAY CAKE BANANA BREAD

TOTAL TIME: 1 HR 15 MIN / SERVES 6

Repeat after us: Sprinkles make e-v-e-r-y-t-h-i-n-g better. This is our perfected banana bread base: It's not too sweet, never dry, and stupid-addictive.

½ cup (1 stick) melted butter, plus more for pan

1 cup all-purpose flour, plus more for pan

1 teaspoon baking soda

¼ teaspoon kosher salt

¾ cup sugar

¼ cup buttermilk

1 teaspoon pure vanilla extract

1 large egg

1 large egg yolk

3 super-ripe bananas, mashed with a fork

½ cup white chocolate chips

½ cup rainbow sprinkles

Vanilla Glaze

1. Preheat oven to 350°F and butter and flour a 9x5-inch loaf pan.

2. In a large bowl, whisk together flour, baking soda, and salt.

3. In another large bowl, combine sugar, melted butter, buttermilk, vanilla, egg, and egg yolk until smooth. Pour wet ingredients over dry and stir until combined, then fold in mashed bananas and white chocolate chips. Gently fold in sprinkles and transfer batter to prepared pan.

4. Bake until deeply golden and a toothpick inserted into center comes out clean, about 1 hour.

5. Let bread cool in pan 10 minutes, then invert onto a wire rack to cool completely.

6. Drizzle Vanilla Glaze over bread before slicing.

NO BUTTERMILK? Sub in the same amount of milk mixed with a squeeze of lemon juice, or mix together equal parts milk and plain yogurt.

VANILLA GLAZE

In a small bowl, stir together ½ cup
POWDERED SUGAR, 1 tablespoon **MILK**,
and ½ teaspoon **PURE VANILLA EXTRACT**
until smooth. (Add more **MILK** 1 teaspoon
at a time until pourable.)

Our favorite way to **SEPARATE EGGS** is by simply cracking the egg and separating the yolk back and forth, but you can also use the water bottle hack: Crack an egg into a bowl and use an empty plastic bottle to suction the yolk inside. (It's kinda crazy how well it works.)

CLOUD EGGS

TOTAL TIME: 20 MIN / SERVES 4

At first we dismissed these as an overblown Pinterest trend—until we tried them and fell for the hype. The low-carb poufs are made by whipping egg whites into "clouds," then spooning over a yolk and baking until set. Ham and a little Parm add the salty kick they need.

8 large eggs

1 cup freshly grated Parmesan

½ pound deli ham, chopped

Kosher salt

Freshly ground black pepper

Freshly chopped chives, for garnish

1. Preheat oven to 450°F and grease a large baking sheet with cooking spray.

2. Separate egg whites and yolks, placing egg whites in a large bowl and yolks in a small bowl. Using a whisk or hand mixer, beat egg whites until stiff peaks form Ⓐ, 3 minutes. Gently fold in Parmesan and ham and season with salt and pepper.

3. Spoon 8 mounds of egg whites onto prepared baking sheet and indent centers to form nests Ⓑ. Bake until lightly golden Ⓒ, about 3 minutes.

4. Carefully spoon an egg yolk into center of each nest Ⓓ and season with salt and pepper. Bake until yolks are just set, about 3 minutes more.

5. Garnish with chives before serving.

— WATCH & LEARN —

Ⓐ   Ⓑ   Ⓒ   Ⓓ

CHICKS & WAFFLES

TOTAL TIME: 45 MIN / SERVES 6

Reignite your love of toaster waffles with these adorable breakfast sliders. If you really want to show off, skip the maple syrup and serve with Hot Honey (see page 248).

1 cup all-purpose flour

2 teaspoons kosher salt

1 large egg

1 cup buttermilk (see Tip, page 284)

1½ cups panko breadcrumbs

1 pound boneless, skinless chicken breasts, cut into 1-inch-thick nuggets

Vegetable oil, for frying

12 frozen mini waffles, toasted

2 tablespoons melted butter

Maple syrup, for drizzling

1. In a shallow bowl, whisk together flour and salt. In another shallow bowl, whisk together egg and buttermilk. Put breadcrumbs in a third shallow bowl. Working in batches, dredge chicken pieces in flour mixture, then dip in buttermilk mixture and toss in breadcrumbs until fully coated.

2. In a large deep-sided skillet over medium heat, heat 1½ inches oil until it starts to bubble. Using tongs and working in batches, add 3 or 4 chicken pieces and cook until golden and cooked through, 2 to 3 minutes per side. (Do not crowd the pan, or oil will cool!) Drain on a paper towel–lined wire rack.

3. Brush toasted mini waffles with melted butter. Top half with fried chicken and drizzle with maple syrup. Sandwich with remaining waffles.

4. Insert toothpick into center of each waffle slider and serve.

YOU'LL CLUCKING LOVE THESE A WAFFLE LOT.

EVERYTHING BAGEL DIP

TOTAL TIME: 20 MIN / SERVES 8

Everything bagels are our everything—but not everyone wants to chow down on a whole bagel. This is our solution to snacking on the flavor without all the carbs.

2 (8-ounce) blocks cream cheese, softened

2 tablespoons minced onion

2 teaspoons garlic powder

2 teaspoons poppy seeds

2 teaspoons sesame seeds

Kosher salt

Freshly ground black pepper

Plain bagel chips, for serving

1. In a large bowl using a hand mixer, beat cream cheese, onion, garlic powder, poppy seeds, and sesame seeds until fluffy and combined. Season with salt and pepper.

2. Refrigerate 30 minutes to let flavors meld.

3. Serve with bagel chips.

 EVERYTHING SEASONING is becoming so popular you can buy it pre-mixed if you don't want to make your own.

WTF?

EVERYTHING BAGEL PIZZA

THE PARLOR / Dobbs Ferry, NY

Everything seasoning may be having a moment, but New Yorkers have been sprinkling the stuff on more than just bagels long before grocery stores starting bottling it. At The Parlor in Dobbs Ferry, New York, the seed-filled mix is the star of one of the joint's most popular pizzas. Chefs top the pie with house-made mozzarella, a little Parmesan, and an egg that's strategically cracked in the middle, so every slice has some ooey-gooey yolk. The everything seasoning—sea salt, garlic, onion, caraway seeds, poppy seeds, and sesame seeds—comes after the pizza's been cooked. People clamor for a taste of it first thing in the morning . . . which comes as no surprise to chef David DiBari. The dish is based on his favorite hangover food: "My dirty-shame place is an everything bagel with cream cheese and an egg," he laughs.

BOSTON CREAM PANCAKES

TOTAL TIME: 35 MIN / SERVES 4

We've never met a Boston cream pie we didn't like—which is why we decided to push the dessert into breakfast territory. This decadent recipe uses pancake and yellow cake mix for a little more sweetness. If you don't want to bother with a ganache, melted chocolate chips are a fine sub.

FOR THE PANCAKES
Cooking spray

1 cup pancake mix

1 cup boxed vanilla cake mix

2 large eggs

1 cup milk

1 teaspoon pure vanilla extract

FOR THE CREAM FILLING
1 (3.4-ounce) package instant vanilla
  pudding mix

2 cups cold milk

FOR THE GANACHE
¾ cup semisweet chocolate chips

¾ cup heavy cream

1. Make pancakes: Lightly grease a large nonstick skillet with cooking spray and set over medium heat. In a large bowl, whisk together pancake mix, cake mix, eggs, milk, and vanilla until smooth. Using a ¼-cup measure, pour batter into pan to form pancakes. Cook until small bubbles form in batter and pancakes are lightly golden on both sides, 2 to 3 minutes per side. Repeat, regreasing pan when necessary.

2. Make cream filling: In a large bowl, whisk together pudding mix and milk until combined. Let sit until set, 5 minutes.

3. Make ganache: Place chocolate chips in a medium heatproof bowl. Heat cream over medium-low heat until it starts to simmer. Pour over chocolate and let sit 5 minutes, then whisk until completely melted and combined.

4. Assemble pancakes: Make four separate pancake stacks with a layer of pudding in between each pancake and drizzle each with ganache.

6 WAYS TO MAKE MIMOSAS

Because brunch without bubbly is just breakfast.

1

TEQUILA SUNRISE

TEQUILA + BUBBLY +
ORANGE JUICE + GRENADINE +
SUGAR RIM +
ORANGE WEDGE

2

CREAMSICLE

ORANGE JUICE +
BUBBLY + HEAVY CREAM +
ORANGE WEDGE

3

PIÑA COLADA

PINEAPPLE JUICE +
COCONUT RUM + BUBBLY +
PINEAPPLE WEDGE +
MARASCHINO CHERRY

4

LEMONADE

LEMONADE + BUBBLY +
LEMON SLICE

5

CARAMEL APPLE

APPLE CIDER +
CARAMEL VODKA +
BUBBLY + APPLE SLICE +
CINNAMON SUGAR RIM

6

MOSCOW MULE

GINGER BEER + VODKA +
BUBBLY + ORANGE JUICE +
SUGAR RIM + LIME SLICE

> Jo and I decided to host a Facebook Live on mimosas. When we went to open the first bottle of champagne, the cork flew off and champagne started flying everywhere. We laughed it off, but then the next TWO we grabbed did the exact same thing. We're already the most dramatic Delish staffers, so the video turned into us covered in champagne, screaming and cry-laughing. —FUNS

TEQUILA
SUNRISE
MIMOSAS

CHILAMIGAS

TOTAL TIME: 35 MIN / SERVES 4 TO 6

We couldn't decide whether *chilaquiles* or *migas* deserved a spot in the book, so we fused the two to create this Tex-Mex mess. If you've never made eggs with tortilla chips before, you're truly missing out; the chips soften and add a subtle salty crunch. You can definitely poach the eggs right in the tomato sauce, but we always end up missing the crispy texture of fried ones.

3 tablespoons extra-virgin olive oil, divided

1 medium onion, chopped

1 jalapeño, finely chopped

2 cloves garlic, minced

1 (28-ounce) can crushed tomatoes

Kosher salt

Freshly ground black pepper

4 cups tortilla chips

4 to 6 large eggs

Crumbled cotija, for serving

Freshly chopped cilantro, for serving

Sour cream, for drizzling

1. In a large skillet over medium heat, heat 2 tablespoons of oil. Add onion and jalapeño and cook, stirring, until soft, 5 minutes. Add garlic and cook until fragrant, 1 minute more. Add tomatoes and bring to a simmer, stirring often, until reduced, 8 to 10 minutes. (If mixture seems too dry, add a splash of water.)

2. Season sauce generously with salt and pepper. Add tortilla chips and toss gently with sauce to cover and soften. Turn off heat.

3. Meanwhile, in a large nonstick skillet over medium heat, heat remaining 1 tablespoon oil and fry eggs to your liking.

4. Top chip mixture with fried egg, cotija, cilantro, and sour cream.

BREAKFAST-STUFFED BAGUETTE

TOTAL TIME: 50 MIN / SERVES 4

Basically a frittata in a bread bowl. It hits all the notes of a breakfast sandwich, only with way cooler presentation. Cut into thick slices and your friends won't know how to react.

4 slices bacon

2 medium baguettes

8 large eggs

⅓ cup heavy cream

1 cup shredded white cheddar cheese

2 green onions, thinly sliced

Kosher salt

Freshly ground black pepper

1. Preheat oven to 350°F and line a large baking sheet with parchment paper.

2. In a large nonstick skillet over medium heat, cook bacon until crispy, 8 minutes. Drain on a paper towel-lined plate, then chop.

3. Cut a deep V through the top of each baguette and partially unstuff bread. Transfer baguettes, V-side up, to prepared baking sheet.

4. In a large bowl, whisk together eggs and heavy cream, then stir in bacon, cheddar cheese, and green onions and season with salt and pepper. Pour mixture into each baguette boat.

5. Bake until eggs are puffy and set in center, 30 minutes.

6. Let cool 10 minutes before slicing.

Look for **SMALL BAGUETTES** that can lay fully flat on your baking sheet. The egg mixture tends to spill over.

CHOCOLATE CHIP PANCAKE BAKE

TOTAL TIME: 5 HRS 20 MIN / SERVES 8

This was the first-ever brunch recipe we made at Delish, and it's the perfect dish for a crowd: You bake cooked pancakes in an egg mixture, and they become the fluffiest version of themselves. Prep it the night before (the overnight soak = worth it) and bake in the a.m.

Butter, for baking dish

20 cooked pancakes (fresh or thawed frozen)

5 large eggs

2 cups milk (preferably whole or 2%)

¼ cup sugar

1 teaspoon pure vanilla extract

½ cup semisweet chocolate chips

Powdered sugar, for serving

Maple syrup, for serving

1. Butter a large baking dish. Cut cooked pancakes in half and begin fanning them out, round-side up, in the dish.

2. In a large bowl, whisk together eggs, milk, sugar, and vanilla. Pour over pancakes, flattening them with a spatula to make sure they're completely submerged in liquid. Cover with foil and refrigerate at least 4 hours and up to overnight.

3. When ready to bake, preheat oven to 350°F.

4. Sprinkle pancakes with chocolate chips, re-cover with foil, and bake 40 minutes. Remove foil and continue baking until golden and completely cooked through, 10 minutes more.

5. Dust with powdered sugar and serve with maple syrup.

WTF?

STRAWBERRY CHEESECAKE–STUFFED FRENCH TOAST

DELICATESSEN / New York, NY

Anyone who's ever wasted an insane portion of their daily calorie count on a mediocre brunch can relate to chef Michael Ferraro's stance on French toast: "It's one of those things that I will only order if I know it'll be ridiculously good," he explains. "Otherwise, why wouldn't I just have an egg white omelet?" That's how he came to develop the French toast for Delicatessen in New York City. It's incredibly decadent for a first-thing-in-the-morning dish: a giant hunk of brioche piped full of strawberry cream cheese filling. The whole thing's deep-fried like a donut but topped with syrup and cut fruit, as is traditional for a plate of French toast. It's a hulking masterpiece, but Ferraro feels only sincere admiration for—not judgment toward—anyone who licks the plate clean. "We had a group of four tiny girls come in recently who all ordered entrées—burgers and Benedicts—and a French toast appetizer for the table," he remembers. "I was like, 'I might love these girls!'"

CHURRO FRENCH TOAST

TOTAL TIME: 25 MIN / SERVES 4

Churro is a verb at Delish—we've churro'd nachos, bananas, and now French toast. This is obviously not an everyday breakfast; we like to make it when there's something to celebrate. Kinda-stale white sandwich bread is always great, but brioche or challah are even better.

1 tablespoon butter

6 large eggs

1½ cups whole milk

1 tablespoon pure vanilla extract

Kosher salt

1 cup cinnamon sugar

8 slices white bread

Insane Icing

1. In a large nonstick skillet over medium heat, melt butter. In a shallow bowl, whisk together eggs, milk, vanilla, and a pinch of salt. Put cinnamon sugar in another shallow bowl.

2. Dip 2 slices bread into egg mixture until soaked through, then add to skillet and cook until golden, about 2 minutes per side. Remove from skillet and immediately toss in cinnamon sugar. Transfer to a wire rack to cool and crisp up while you cook remaining bread slices.

3. Drizzle French toast with Insane Icing before serving.

INSANE ICING

In a liquid measuring cup, whisk together 2 tablespoons **SOFTENED CREAM CHEESE**, ¼ cup **POWDERED SUGAR**, and 1 tablespoon **MILK** until smooth.

DIY AVOCADO TOAST

TOTAL TIME: 10 MIN / SERVES 6

If we all love to 'gram avocado toast so much, how come we forget all about it on a brunch spread? We like to put out a big bowl of mashed avos with bagel chips (or crostini, page 71) and let people dig in, guac-style.

4 avocados

Juice of 1 lemon

Kosher salt

Freshly ground black pepper

Pinch crushed red pepper flakes

Extra-virgin olive oil, for drizzling

Flaky sea salt

Bagel chips, for serving

1. In a large bowl, mash avocados and lemon juice with a fork. Season with salt, pepper, and red pepper flakes.

2. Transfer to a serving bowl, drizzle with oil, and sprinkle with flaky sea salt. Serve with bagel chips.

BACON PANCAKE DIPPERS

DELISH FAVE

TOTAL TIME: 20 MIN / SERVES 6

Admit it: When pouring syrup over pancakes, you always let a little get on your bacon, too. We can't believe it took us so many years to figure out this salty-sweet lovechild. Put them out and let your friends discover the bacon surprise inside.

12 slices bacon, halved

2 cups pancake mix, plus ingredients called for on box

3 tablespoons butter, divided

Maple syrup, for serving

1. In a large nonstick skillet over medium heat, cook bacon until crispy, 8 minutes. Drain on a paper towel-lined plate. Discard fat and wipe skillet clean.

2. Meanwhile, prepare pancake batter according to box instructions.

3. Add 1 tablespoon butter to same skillet over medium heat and melt.

4. Using tongs, coat each bacon half in pancake batter. Working in batches, add battered bacon to skillet and cook until bubbles begin to form on surface of batter, about 2 minutes. Flip and cook 2 minutes more. Repeat until all bacon dippers are cooked, adding more butter to skillet as needed between batches.

5. Serve bacon dippers with maple syrup.

You can turn ANYTHING into pancake dippers; we love battering breakfast sausage, apple slices, and bananas.

Hollandaise sauce **IS FINICKY:** Don't heat it too much or else the eggs will start scrambling (worst nightmare). Make sure the bowl never touches the water, and don't stop whisking.

EGGS BENEDICT BAKE

TOTAL TIME: 2 HRS 30 MIN / SERVES 6

For years we assumed that making eggs Benny at home wasn't worth it—restaurants could always do it better. This layered casserole debunks that. You don't even have to poach eggs; instead, you deconstruct the dish and layer up the ingredients in one skillet.

Butter, for skillet

8 English muffins, torn into small pieces

1 pound sliced deli ham, chopped

8 large eggs

2 cups whole milk

1 teaspoon garlic powder

Kosher salt

Freshly ground black pepper

FOR THE HOLLANDAISE

4 large egg yolks

Juice of ½ lemon

½ cup (1 stick) melted butter

Pinch cayenne pepper

Paprika, for garnish

1. Butter a large oven-safe skillet. Alternate layers of English muffins and ham in skillet until they're both used up.

2. In a large bowl, whisk together eggs, milk, and garlic powder and season generously with salt and pepper. Pour mixture over ingredients in skillet and cover with plastic wrap. Refrigerate at least 1 hour or up to overnight.

3. When ready to bake, preheat oven to 375°F.

4. Bake until bread is golden and eggs are cooked through, 1 hour. (Cover with foil if top is getting too brown.) Let cool.

5. Make hollandaise: Bring 2 inches of water to a boil in a small saucepan, then reduce heat to maintain a low simmer. In a medium heatproof bowl, whisk together egg yolks with lemon juice. Place over saucepan (be sure bottom of bowl doesn't touch water) and, while whisking vigorously, slowly add melted butter and whisk until thickened, about 2 minutes. Remove from heat and season with cayenne and salt.

6. Drizzle hollandaise over bake and sprinkle with paprika before serving.

PUMPKIN SPICE PULL-APART BREAD

TOTAL TIME: 1 HR / SERVES 8

Pumpkin spice is a season at Delish; we start adding the cinnamon-nutmeg blend to pretty much everything when it's still 90 degrees outside. This pull-apart bread uses one of our favorite hacks for store-bought biscuits: stacking them with a filling and baking in a loaf pan.

Butter, for pan

1 cup sugar

1½ teaspoons pumpkin pie spice, divided

1 (16-ounce) can refrigerated biscuits, halved lengthwise

1 cup pumpkin puree

½ teaspoon pure vanilla extract

FOR THE GLAZE

¼ (8-ounce) block cream cheese, softened

½ cup powdered sugar

½ teaspoon pure vanilla extract

¼ teaspoon pumpkin pie spice

¼ cup milk

1. Preheat oven to 350°F and butter a 9x5-inch loaf pan.

2. Pour sugar and 1 teaspoon of pumpkin pie spice into a large resealable plastic bag and shake to combine. Add biscuit pieces to bag 2 or 3 at a time, seal, and shake until coated. Set coated biscuit pieces aside on a plate and repeat with remaining pieces.

3. In a medium bowl, combine pumpkin puree, vanilla, and remaining ½ teaspoon pumpkin pie spice. Slather pumpkin filling on a biscuit, then top with another biscuit and slather with more filling. Repeat until you've created a stack of biscuits (or two stacks of biscuits).

4. Place biscuit stack on its side in prepared pan, so you see layers of pumpkin filling.

5. Bake until biscuits are golden and puffed, 38 to 40 minutes. Let cool slightly, then turn out onto a plate.

6. Make glaze: In a large bowl using a hand mixer on low speed, beat cream cheese until light and fluffy. Add powdered sugar, vanilla, and pumpkin pie spice and mix until combined, then gradually add milk and beat until it's a pourable consistency.

7. Drizzle glaze over pull-apart bread before serving.

 This method also works with **SAVORY BREADS:** Layer your favorite spinach dip (obviously the one on page 75) between biscuits and bake until bubbly.

COWBOY BREAKFAST SKILLET

TOTAL TIME: 1 HR 10 MIN / SERVES 8

This is basically a frittata on steroids—loaded with potatoes, black beans, and two types of cheese. You cook the potatoes and peppers in bacon fat—because bacon—so they take on an extra savory, smoky flavor.

6 slices bacon

2 medium russet potatoes, peeled and diced

1 red bell pepper, chopped

1 green bell pepper, chopped

½ medium onion, chopped

1 cup canned black beans, drained and rinsed

3 green onions, thinly sliced

½ teaspoon chili powder

¼ teaspoon paprika

Kosher salt

Freshly ground black pepper

10 large eggs

¼ cup half-and-half

¾ cup shredded cheddar cheese

¾ cup shredded Monterey jack cheese

Hot sauce, for serving

1. Preheat oven to 350°F.

2. In a large oven-safe skillet over medium heat, cook bacon until crispy, 8 minutes. Drain on a paper towel–lined plate, then chop. Pour off all but 2 tablespoons fat from skillet.

3. Add potatoes, bell peppers, and onions to skillet and stir until coated. Cook, stirring occasionally, until soft, about 5 minutes.

4. Pour ¼ cup water over vegetables and cover skillet with a large lid. Cook, stirring occasionally, until potatoes are fork-tender, about 15 minutes.

5. Stir in black beans, green onions, chili powder, paprika, and bacon and season with salt and pepper.

6. In a large bowl, whisk together eggs and half-and-half. Stir in half of both cheeses and season with salt and pepper. Pour mixture over skillet and gently stir to combine, then sprinkle with remaining cheese.

7. Bake until eggs are puffy and set, about 30 minutes.

8. Let cool 10 minutes, then serve with hot sauce.

BANANA BREAD WAFFLES

TOTAL TIME: 30 MIN / SERVES 6

We really love banana bread, but frankly, the cooking world doesn't do enough with the batter. We put it in a waffle maker—it's basically our dream breakfast.

Cooking spray

2 cups all-purpose flour

1 teaspoon baking soda

½ teaspoon kosher salt

½ cup (1 stick) melted butter

1 cup sugar

1 large egg

1 large egg yolk

¼ cup sour cream

1 teaspoon pure vanilla extract

3 ripe bananas, mashed with a fork

1 cup semisweet chocolate chips

Maple syrup, for serving

1. Heat waffle iron and grease with cooking spray.

2. In a large bowl, whisk together flour, baking soda, and salt.

3. In another large bowl, stir together melted butter, sugar, egg, egg yolk, sour cream, and vanilla. Add mashed bananas and stir until combined. Gradually add dry ingredients to wet ingredients until just combined. Fold in chocolate chips.

4. Add ¼ cup batter to waffle iron. Close and cook until golden on both sides. Transfer waffle to a plate and repeat with remaining batter.

5. Serve with maple syrup.

CHAPTER ELEVEN

THERE'S ALWAYS ROOM...

Because skipping dessert is for quitters.

COOKIEDILLA

TOTAL TIME: 20 MIN / MAKES 1

When you work at a place like Delish, your mind is constantly mulling over very important questions like, "What else could form a quesadilla besides a tortilla?!" When we realized giant chocolate chip cookies not only work but dominate, we cried—then stuffed marshmallow and chocolate sauce inside and cried some more.

½ **(16.5-ounce) package refrigerated chocolate chip cookie dough**

½ **cup marshmallow creme**

½ **cup chocolate fudge sauce**

1. Preheat oven to 350°F and line a baking sheet with parchment paper.

2. Divide cookie dough into 2 balls and place on separate sides of prepared baking sheet. Flatten into big disks.

3. Bake until golden and cooked through, 15 to 20 minutes. (Now is not the time for an underbaked, gooey center!) Let cool on baking sheet 10 minutes, then transfer to a wire rack and let cool completely. Keep oven on.

4. Spread marshmallow creme on bottom of one cookie. Spread chocolate fudge sauce on bottom of other cookie and place, chocolate-side down, on top of marshmallow creme.

5. Return to oven and bake until warmed through, 3 to 4 minutes.

6. Slice and serve.

NUTELLA-STUFFED COOKIES

TOTAL TIME: 1 HR 25 MIN / MAKES 2 DOZEN

We don't know what makes these so good. The cookie is softer than it probably should be, the chocolate flavor is almost too rich, and the warm Nutella filling stays magically melty long after they come out of the oven. But it might also be the flaky sea salt . . .

1½ cups Nutella

1 cup (2 sticks) butter, softened

1 cup packed brown sugar

½ cup sugar

2 large eggs

2 tablespoons milk

2 teaspoons pure vanilla extract

2 cups all-purpose flour

1 cup unsweetened dark cocoa powder

1 teaspoon baking soda

1 teaspoon kosher salt

Flaky sea salt

1. Line a baking sheet with parchment paper. Scoop 1-tablespoon balls of Nutella onto prepared baking sheet (24 balls total).

2. In a large bowl using a hand mixer, beat butter and both sugars until light and fluffy. Add eggs, milk, and vanilla and beat until combined, then add flour, cocoa powder, baking soda, and salt. Refrigerate dough while Nutella is in freezer.

3. Preheat oven to 350°F and line a baking sheet with parchment paper.

4. Scoop a heaping tablespoon of cookie dough and flatten into a pancake-like circle. Top with a frozen Nutella ball and cover with dough, pinching to seal and adding more dough if necessary to completely cover. Transfer to prepared baking sheet and repeat with remaining dough and frozen Nutella, spacing cookies 2 inches apart.

5. Sprinkle cookies with flaky sea salt and bake until puffed, 15 minutes. Let cool on pan 5 minutes before serving.

You can also **FREEZE** disks of Nutella and use them to stuff pancakes.

SNICKERDOODLE BLONDIES

TOTAL TIME: 45 MIN / MAKES 16

Blondies have more fun—but that's not the only reason to bake snickerdoodles like this: The fudgy inside and crackly topping make each square taste like a churro disguised as the softest cookie ever.

Cooking spray

¾ cup (1½ sticks) butter, softened

1 cup sugar

½ cup packed brown sugar

2 large eggs

2 teaspoons pure vanilla extract

2 cups all-purpose flour

1 teaspoon ground cinnamon

¾ teaspoon baking powder

½ teaspoon kosher salt

2 tablespoons cinnamon sugar

1. Preheat oven to 350°F and grease a 9x9-inch pan with cooking spray.

2. In a large bowl using a hand mixer, beat butter and both sugars until light and fluffy. Add eggs and vanilla and beat until combined.

3. In another bowl, whisk together flour, cinnamon, baking powder, and salt. Add dry ingredients to wet ingredients and beat until just combined.

4. Press batter into prepared pan and sprinkle top with cinnamon sugar. Bake until golden and still slightly soft in the middle, 25 to 30 minutes.

5. Let cool completely before slicing into squares.

 SNICKERDOODLE PURISTS were pissed these don't have cream of tartar, but trust us: They have the perfect amount of chew without it.

GIANT TWINKIE CAKE

TOTAL TIME: 1 HR 20 MIN / SERVES 8 TO 10

When Jo threw out the idea of a giant Twinkie baked in a Bundt pan, you can only imagine the raised eyebrows she got. Thank God she did—dense pound cake + marshmallow buttercream = heaven.

FOR THE CAKE

Cooking spray

All-purpose flour, for pan

1 (15-ounce) box vanilla cake mix

1 (3.4-ounce) package vanilla instant pudding mix

4 large eggs

½ cup (1 stick) melted butter

FOR THE FILLING

½ cup (1 stick) butter, softened

1 (7.5-ounce) jar marshmallow creme

3 cups powdered sugar

1 teaspoon pure vanilla extract

2 to 4 tablespoons heavy cream

1. Preheat oven to 350°F. Grease a Bundt pan with cooking spray (be generous!) and dust with flour, tapping out any excess.

2. In a large bowl using a hand mixer, beat cake mix, pudding mix, eggs, melted butter, and 1 cup water until smooth and combined.

3. Pour batter into prepared pan and bake until a toothpick inserted into cake comes out clean, about 45 minutes.

4. Let cake cool in pan 10 minutes, then invert onto a wire rack to cool completely. Carefully place back in Bundt pan.

5. Make filling: In a large bowl using a hand mixer, beat butter until light and fluffy, then add marshmallow creme, powdered sugar, and vanilla and beat until smooth. Gradually add heavy cream if mixture is too stiff and transfer to a large piping bag or resealable plastic bag with the end snipped.

6. Using a teaspoon, scoop out 8 to 10 large holes around bottom of cake, making sure not to cut through the top (Ⓐ,Ⓑ).

7. Pipe filling into holes Ⓒ, then carefully invert cake onto a serving platter Ⓓ and dust with powdered sugar.

WATCH & LEARN

Ⓐ Ⓑ Ⓒ Ⓓ

COOKIE DOUGH CHEESECAKE

TOTAL TIME: 7 HRS / SERVES 10 TO 12

Holy s*it: Chocolate chip cookie crust, cookie dough filling and frosting, crushed cookie sides. This labor of love (yes, we recommend a water bath) is ALWAYS the center of attention.

FOR THE CRUST

Butter, for pan

1 log refrigerated chocolate chip cookie dough, divided

FOR THE CHEESECAKE

4 (8-ounce) blocks cream cheese, softened

1¼ cups sugar

½ teaspoons kosher salt

4 large eggs, room temperature

½ cup sour cream

¼ cup heavy cream

1 tablespoon pure vanilla extract

¾ cup mini chocolate chips, divided

1. Make crust: Preheat oven to 350°F. Butter a 9-inch springform pan and wrap bottom and sides of pan in a double layer of aluminum foil.

2. Pat ¾ of the cookie dough log into bottom of prepared pan. Bake until golden, 26 minutes. Let cool. Reduce oven temperature to 325°F.

3. Make cheesecake: In a large bowl using a hand mixer, or in bowl of a stand mixer using paddle attachment, beat cream cheese until completely smooth, 3 minutes. Add sugar and salt and beat until fluffy, 2 minutes more. Add eggs, one at a time, beating after each addition and scraping down bowl as necessary. Add sour cream, heavy cream, and vanilla and beat, 1 minute more.

4. Pour half of cheesecake batter on top of crust, then sprinkle with half of chocolate chips. Roll remaining cookie dough into tiny balls and drop on top of cheesecake. Repeat with remaining batter and chocolate chips.

5. Bring a medium saucepan of water to a boil. Place cheesecake in a deep roasting pan and set on middle rack of oven. Carefully pour enough boiling water into roasting pan to come halfway up sides of springform pan.

RECIPE CONTINUES ➜

FOR THE FROSTING

½ (8-ounce) block cream cheese, softened

4 tablespoons (½ stick) butter, softened

¼ cup powdered sugar

2 tablespoons brown sugar

½ teaspoon pure vanilla extract

½ teaspoon kosher salt

½ cup mini chocolate chips

FOR DECORATING

3 chocolate chip cookies, halved

2 cups broken chocolate chip cookies

6. Bake until cheesecake is just starting to brown and only the center is slightly jiggly, about 2 hours. Turn off oven, prop open the door with a wooden spoon, and let cheesecake slowly cool in its water bath, 1 hour.

7. Remove roasting pan from oven, then carefully lift springform pan from water and remove foil. Set cheesecake on a rack and let come to room temperature. Once completely cool, loosely cover with plastic wrap and refrigerate until firm, 4 hours or up to overnight. When ready to serve, carefully unmold from springform pan.

8. Make frosting: In a large bowl using a hand mixer, beat cream cheese, butter, powdered sugar, brown sugar, vanilla, and salt. Fold in chocolate chips.

9. Dollop frosting on top of cheesecake in 6 mounds and top each with a cookie half, then cover cheesecake sides with crushed cookies.

 WATER BATHS can be a drag, but they do help prevent cheesecakes from cracking. If you're not using a topping, don't skip this step.

COOKIES 'N' CREAM BROWNIES

TOTAL TIME: 1 HR / MAKES 16

We're suckers for anything cookies 'n' cream, but these Oreo-stuffed brownies are on another level. The "frosting" is actually melted Hershey's Cookies 'n' Creme bars. (Whoever can have just one bite of these, call us—we want to know what superpower you have.)

---

1 (18-ounce) box brownie mix, plus ingredients called for on box

16 Oreos

4 Hershey's Cookies 'n' Creme bars

Melted chocolate, for drizzling (optional)

1. Preheat oven to 350°F and line a 8x8-inch pan with parchment paper.

2. Prepare brownie batter according to package instructions. Pour batter into prepared pan, then top with an even layer of Oreos. Press down on Oreos so batter covers them almost completely.

3. Bake until a toothpick inserted into center comes out mostly clean, about 35 minutes. Let cool completely.

4. Place unwrapped candy bars in a medium microwave-safe bowl. Microwave until melted, about 3 minutes. Pour over cooled brownie and, using an offset spatula, smooth into an even layer.

5. Refrigerate until set, 10 minutes, then drizzle with melted chocolate, if using, and slice into squares.

Make these even MORE INSANE: Bake the brownie in an oven-safe skillet and top with a few scoops of vanilla ice cream before handing out spoons.

UNCORN BARK

TOTAL TIME: 1 HR 15 MIN / SERVES 8

If you've never unicorned anything, you're missing out. This white chocolate bark is all about the simple swirling technique, which makes the whole thing so magical.

5 cups white chocolate chips, melted

Pink food coloring

Yellow food coloring

Purple food coloring

Blue food coloring

Sprinkles and candy pearls

1. Divide melted chocolate among four bowls. Add a different color food coloring to each bowl and stir until combined.

2. Line a baking sheet with parchment paper and drop spoonfuls of each color chocolate in a collage-like pattern, working out from middle of baking sheet.

3. Using an offset spatula, mix colors together to make a swirling pattern (be careful not to overmix) and fill tray.

4. Top all over with sprinkles and candy pearls.

5. Refrigerate 1 hour, then break bark into pieces before serving.

Most of the time we don't fuss with piping tips. We like to put the frosting in a resealable **PLASTIC BAG** and snip off a lot of the corner so we have a wide opening that's super easy to maneuver.

MARGARITA CUPCAKES

Who knew swapping out milk for tequila in buttercream was the best idea ever? This is our favorite vanilla cake recipe—not at all dry—but you can also just fold the juice and zest of a lime into a box mix and fool everyone that they're 100% homemade.

FOR THE CUPCAKES

1 cup (2 sticks) butter, softened

1½ cups sugar

3 large eggs

Juice of 3 limes, plus zest of 1 lime

1 teaspoon pure vanilla extract

2 cups all-purpose flour

3 tablespoons cornstarch

1½ teaspoons baking powder

1 teaspoon kosher salt

½ cup milk (preferably whole or 2%)

FOR THE FROSTING

1 cup (2 sticks) butter, softened

5 cups powdered sugar

¼ cup fresh lime juice

¼ cup tequila

Coarse salt, for garnish

Lime zest, for garnish

Small lime wedges, for garnish

1. Make cupcakes: Preheat oven to 350°F and line two muffin tins with 18 cupcake liners.

2. In a large bowl using a hand mixer, beat butter and sugar until light and fluffy. Add eggs, one at a time, beating well after each addition. Add lime juice and zest and vanilla and mix until combined.

3. In another large bowl, whisk together flour, cornstarch, baking powder, and salt. Add half the dry ingredients to the wet ingredients, beating until just combined. Pour in milk and mix until fully incorporated. Add remaining dry ingredients and stir until just combined. Fill cupcake liners ¾ full with batter.

4. Bake until slightly golden and a toothpick inserted into center of each cupcake comes out clean, about 25 minutes. Let cupcakes cool in pans 5 to 10 minutes, then transfer to a wire rack to cool completely.

5. Make frosting: In a large bowl using a hand mixer, beat butter, half of powdered sugar, lime juice, and tequila until light and fluffy. Add remaining powdered sugar and beat until smooth.

6. Pipe frosting onto cooled cupcakes. Garnish with coarse salt, lime zest, and lime wedges and a cut decorative straw before serving.

WTF?

CLOUD CONES

MILK TRAIN / London, England

The lyrics "I scream, you scream, we all scream for ice cream!" could be Milk Train Café's anthem. Tweens, hipsters, and grandmas alike literally squeal when they're handed the scoop shop's signature creation called a Cloud Cone. It's an ice cream cone wrapped in a pillowy "cloud" of cotton candy, and you can get it sprinkled with even more candy and syrup. Have your phone at the ready: The treat has become one of the most Instagrammed desserts in the world. And there's no doubt why. Since the London-based ice cream shop opened in August 2016, there's been a line around the block for their over-the-top concessions. "We spin so much cotton candy every day, it could fill our entire shop," says owner Mike Tran. But instead of turning the stuff into decoration, he puts it to good use: Employees sling about four hundred Cloud Cones a day—twice that when it's super busy with throngs of tourists.

GIANT CHIPWICH

TOTAL TIME: 3 HRS 30 MIN / SERVES 10

Memories of flagging down the ice cream truck for this iconic vanilla ice cream–chocolate chip cookie sandwich inspired Jo to do a version the size of a dinner plate for sharing. Every millimeter of ice cream is studded in chocolate chips just like the original.

2 (16.5-ounce) packages refrigerated chocolate chip cookie dough

½ gallon vanilla ice cream, softened (see Tip)

1 cup mini chocolate chips

1. Preheat oven to 350°F and line two 9-inch cake pans with parchment paper.

2. Press 1 package cookie dough into bottom of each prepared pan. Bake until golden, about 20 minutes. Let cool in pans 10 minutes, then remove and freeze 30 minutes.

3. Remove cookies from freezer. Flip one over, flat-side up, and scoop on vanilla ice cream, smoothing top with a spatula to create an even layer. Sandwich with second frozen cookie, flat-side down, pressing to push ice cream out to the sides. Smooth ice cream along sides and press sides in chocolate chips until exposed ice cream is completely covered.

4. Set ice cream sandwich on serving plate and freeze until firm, 2 hours.

5. When ready to serve, remove from freezer to let soften, 10 minutes, then slice like a cake.

 We've suffered too many **MELTY ICE CREAM CAKES** and sandwiches to let you do the same. When making any ice cream dessert, skip "slow-churned" or "extra-smooth" ice creams.

BIRTHDAY CAKE FUDGE

TOTAL TIME: 2 HRS 15 MIN / MAKES 16 PIECES

Raise your hand if you'd rather lick the bowl of cake batter or eat just the frosting off a cupcake. This four-ingredient fudge fills that void. It also started our love affair with sweetened condensed milk: We're convinced the sticky, syrupy stuff makes everything taste a thousand times better.

1 (14-ounce) can sweetened condensed milk

½ cup yellow or Funfetti cake mix

2 cups white chocolate chips, melted

½ cup confetti rainbow sprinkles, divided

1. Line a 8x8- or 9x9-inch pan with parchment paper.

2. In a large bowl, stir together sweetened condensed milk and cake mix until combined. Fold in melted chocolate. (It may look like chocolate is seizing, but keep stirring until smooth and thick.) Gently fold in ¼ cup of sprinkles.

3. Pour mixture into prepared pan and smooth top with an offset spatula. Top with remaining ¼ cup sprinkles and gently press into fudge.

4. Refrigerate until firm, about 2 hours.

5. Cut into 16 pieces and serve.

S'MORES BAKE

TOTAL TIME: 20 MIN / SERVES 8

We didn't think we could come up with a s'mores dessert that's easier to make than actual s'mores—until this. You just pile marshmallows, chocolate, and graham crackers in a baking dish and set a timer for 10 minutes. Perfect for when you need to feed your friends something sweet but are too lazy to actually bake.

Cooking spray

2 cups marshmallows

6 (1.5-ounce) chocolate bars, broken into squares

1 sleeve graham crackers, broken into rectangles

½ cup semisweet chocolate chips, melted

1. Preheat oven to 400°F and grease a baking dish with cooking spray.

2. Add half of marshmallows to prepared baking dish, then top with half of chocolate squares and half of graham crackers. Repeat.

3. Bake until marshmallows are golden and chocolate squares have melted, about 10 minutes.

4. Drizzle with melted chocolate and serve.

> **Lindsay was helping Lauren test S'mores Cupcakes and they caught fire in the oven. Someone thought it was a good idea to open the door—giving it oxygen—so that the flames were licking the oven above. Four things happened all at once: Lauren grabbed the fire extinguisher, Funs froze in panic screaming, 'I don't know what to do!,' and I grabbed my phone to Snap the whole thing. P.S. None of us know how to use the fire extinguisher. —CHELSEA**

DUNKAROOS
ICE CREAM

8 WAYS TO MAKE NO-CHURN ICE CREAM

No churn = no ice cream maker.

Start with the base: Beat 3 cups **HEAVY CREAM** until stiff peaks form. Fold in 1 (14-ounce) can **SWEETENED CONDENSED MILK**, 1 teaspoon **PURE VANILLA EXTRACT**, and your **DESIRED MIX-INS** (below). Transfer mixture to a 9x5-inch loaf pan and smooth top with a spatula. Freeze until firm, 5 hours.

1 DUNKAROOS

CHOPPED BIRTHDAY CAKE +

TEDDY GRAHAMS +

RAINBOW SPRINKLES +

CREAM CHEESE FROSTING

2 HOT CHOCOLATE

HOT COCOA PACKETS +

MINI MARSHMALLOWS

3 COOKIE MONSTER

CRUSHED CHOCOLATE CHIP COOKIES +

CRUSHED OREO COOKIES +

BLUE FOOD COLORING

4 SAMOA

TOASTED COCONUT +

CRUSHED SHORTBREAD COOKIES +

CARAMEL +

CHOCOLATE SAUCE

5 MUDSLIDE

BAILEYS + KAHLÚA +

CHOPPED CHOCOLATE +

CHOCOLATE SAUCE

6 RED VELVET

CRUMBLED RED VELVET CAKE +

CREAM CHEESE

7 BACON BUTTERSCOTCH

CRUMBLED BACON +

BUTTERSCOTCH SYRUP +

MAPLE SYRUP

8 KEY LIME

CREAM CHEESE +

LIME JUICE AND ZEST +

CRUSHED GRAHAM CRACKERS

PEANUT BUTTER CHOCOLATE TRIFLE

TOTAL TIME: 2 HRS 20 MIN / SERVES 12 TO 14

We're suckers for a trifle. This recipe is all about the peanut butter mousse and chocolate cake—after hanging out in the fridge, the two become one.

Cooking spray

1 (15-ounce) box chocolate cake mix, plus ingredients called for on box

1½ cups creamy peanut butter, plus more melted for drizzling

1 (8-ounce) block cream cheese, softened

1 cup powdered sugar

1 cup heavy cream, divided

1 teaspoon pure vanilla extract

2 (8-ounce) tubs Cool Whip, divided

1½ cups semisweet chocolate chips

Chocolate shavings, for garnish

1. Preheat oven to 350°F. Line two 9-inch cake pans with parchment paper and grease with cooking spray.

2. In a large bowl, prepare cake batter according to box directions and divide between prepared pans.

3. Bake until a toothpick inserted into center of each cake comes out clean, about 25 minutes. Let cakes cool in pans 10 minutes, then invert onto on a wire rack to cool completely. Cut one cake into 1-inch cubes. (Reserve second cake for another use.)

4. Meanwhile, in another large bowl using a hand mixer, beat peanut butter and cream cheese until light and fluffy. Add powdered sugar, ¼ cup of heavy cream, and vanilla and beat until smooth. Fold in 1 cup of Cool Whip until no streaks remain.

5. Put chocolate chips in a large heatproof bowl. In a small saucepan over medium heat, heat remaining ¾ cup heavy cream until steaming and bubbles form around the edge. Pour over chocolate chips and let sit 5 minutes, then whisk until smooth.

6. Assemble trifle: In bottom of a trifle dish, scatter half of chocolate cake cubes. Gently spread half of peanut butter mixture on top, creating an even layer. Top with half of chocolate mixture, then a thick layer of Cool Whip. Repeat layering process.

7. Cover and refrigerate until chilled, at least 1 hour and up to overnight.

8. Drizzle with peanut butter and top with chocolate shavings before serving.

COOKIE DOUGH ICE CREAM SANDWICHES

TOTAL TIME: 5 HRS 25 MIN / MAKES 12

For everyone who would way rather eat cookie dough than cookies (so, everyone), these are your new religion. When testing the easiest way to make these, we couldn't fit anything else in the Delish kitchen freezer—we weren't mad. We like to think the result is pretty brilliant.

1 cup (2 sticks) melted butter

1 cup packed brown sugar

¾ cup sugar

¼ cup milk (preferably whole or 2%)

1 teaspoon pure vanilla extract

2½ cups all-purpose flour

1 teaspoon kosher salt

1½ cups mini chocolate chips

3 quarts vanilla ice cream, softened

1. Line a large baking sheet with parchment paper, leaving overhang on sides.

2. In a large bowl, stir together melted butter, both sugars, milk, and vanilla until combined. Stir in flour and salt, then fold in chocolate chips.

3. Press cookie dough into prepared baking sheet, evening it out as much as possible (a cutting board can help). Top with a second piece of parchment and freeze until firm, 1 hour.

4. Remove cookie dough from pan and place on a cutting board. Slice dough down the center. Scoop ice cream on one half, then gently place other half of cookie dough on top. Transfer back to pan and freeze at least 4 hours and up to overnight.

5. Slice into sandwiches and serve.

Go **GLUTEN-FREE** by subbing in almond flour.

BUTTERBEER PIE

TOTAL TIME: 3 HRS 50 MIN / SERVES 8 TO 10

Making our own Butterbeer, a cult recipe from the world of Harry Potter, was our first super-successful video at Delish: Lindsay concocted it in a plastic cauldron while wearing purple tights, a lacy black top, and a witch hat (we can hardly watch it now, it's so embarrassing). This pie has a butterscotch filling and creamy marshmallow topping, but also a lightning bolt and gold sprinkles because Harry Potter.

FOR THE PIE

2 (14-ounce) refrigerated pie crusts

1½ cups heavy cream

1 (3.4-ounce) package butterscotch instant pudding mix

1½ cups cold milk

¼ cup caramel

FOR THE MARSHMALLOW WHIPPED CREAM

1 cup heavy cream

½ cup marshmallow creme

Gold sprinkles

1. Make pie: Preheat oven to 350°F and line a baking sheet with parchment paper.

2. Unroll one pie crust and drape over a 9-inch pie plate. Fit crust to plate, crimp edges, and prick bottom all over with a fork. Bake until lightly golden, about 18 minutes. (If crust begins to brown too fast, cover edges with foil halfway through.)

3. Meanwhile, cut out a lightning bolt shape from second pie crust and place on prepared baking sheet. Bake until lightly golden, 8 to 10 minutes. Let both crusts cool.

4. In a large bowl using a hand mixer, beat heavy cream until soft peaks form, 6 minutes. In another large bowl, whisk together pudding mix and milk. Let stand until thick, then fold in caramel and whipped cream until combined.

5. Spoon mixture into cooled pie crust and refrigerate until set, about 3 hours.

6. Make marshmallow whipped cream: In a large bowl using a hand mixer, beat heavy cream until soft peaks form, 6 minutes, then fold in marshmallow creme.

7. Spread whipped cream on top of pie and place lightning bolt in center. Decorate with gold sprinkles before serving.

The word **"GANACHE"** sounds fancy, but even the most beginner of cooks can make it. We use the rich chocolate sauce on cakes, cupcakes, and brownies instead of frosting. The ratio of heavy cream to chocolate chips will determine its thickness; 1 part cream to 2 parts chocolate chips is usually perfect.

DING DONG CUPCAKES

TOTAL TIME: 1 HR / MAKES 18

Nostalgia alert: The first sight of this curly icing will send you right back to elementary school. We could eat a whole bowl of the marshmallow filling; it's not too thick and cuts the slight bitterness of the chocolate ganache.

FOR THE CUPCAKES

1 (15-ounce) box devil's food cake mix, plus ingredients called for on box

½ cup (1 stick) butter, softened

2 cups marshmallow creme

1½ cups powdered sugar

½ teaspoon pure vanilla extract

Pinch kosher salt

FOR THE GANACHE AND ICING

2¼ cups semisweet chocolate chips

1 cup heavy cream

1 cup powdered sugar

2 tablespoons milk

1. Preheat oven to 350°F and line two muffin tins with cupcake liners.

2. Prepare cake mix according to box instructions, then fill cupcake liners ¾ full with batter. Bake until a toothpick inserted into center of each cupcake comes out clean, about 25 minutes. Let cupcakes cool in pans 5 to 10 minutes, then transfer to a wire rack to cool completely.

3. Meanwhile, in a large bowl using a hand mixer, beat butter and marshmallow creme until smooth. Add powdered sugar, vanilla, and salt and beat until light and fluffy. Transfer to a pastry bag or large resealable plastic bag with the corner snipped off.

4. Using a teaspoon or melon baller, scoop out a small well from top of each cooled cupcake. Pipe marshmallow filling into each, then smooth top with a butter knife or offset spatula.

5. Make ganache: Put chocolate chips in a large heatproof bowl. In a small saucepan over medium heat, heat heavy cream until steaming and bubbles form around the edge. Pour over chocolate and let sit 5 minutes, then whisk until completely melted and combined.

6. Dip tops of cupcakes in ganache and transfer to a serving plate to let set, 10 minutes.

7. Meanwhile, make icing. In a small bowl, whisk together powdered sugar and milk until smooth. Transfer to a pastry bag or small resealable plastic bag with the corner snipped off.

8. Pipe a decorative doodle pattern across ganache on each cupcake and serve.

NEAPOLITAN CAKE

When Lauren was tasked with making a checkerboard cake, she freaked out. They look impossible, but she nailed it on her first try. To get the stunning patterned look, you just need ample supplies: four cake pans and a set of three different-size biscuit cutters. We love the Neapolitan threesome, but you can use whatever flavor cake mix you want.

Cooking spray

1 (15-ounce) box vanilla cake mix, plus ingredients called for on box

1 (15-ounce) box strawberry cake mix, plus ingredients called for on box

FOR THE FROSTING

1½ cups (3 sticks) butter, softened

3¾ cups powdered sugar

1 cup plus 1 tablespoon unsweetened cocoa powder

1 tablespoon pure vanilla extract

Pinch kosher salt

½ cup heavy cream, plus more if necessary

1. Preheat oven to 350°F. Line four 8-inch round baking pans with parchment paper and grease with cooking spray.

2. Prepare each cake mix in a separate large bowl according to package instructions. Divide batters among prepared pans, making two vanilla cakes and two strawberry cakes.

3. Bake until a toothpick inserted into center of each cake comes out clean, about 25 minutes. Let cakes cool in pans for 10 minutes, then invert onto wire racks to cool completely.

4. Meanwhile, make frosting: In a large bowl using a hand mixer, beat butter, powdered sugar, cocoa powder, vanilla, and salt until light and fluffy. Beat in heavy cream, adding more as needed by the tablespoon until consistency is creamy and spreadable but can still hold peaks, 2 to 3 minutes.

RECIPE CONTINUES

5. When cakes have fully cooled, use a serrated knife to carefully slice off rounded tops. Discard rounded tops and flip cakes over (the bottoms are easier to frost). Use a 6-inch biscuit cutter to gently cut out a large ring from each cake, then use a 4-inch biscuit cutter to cut out a smaller ring from each 6-inch round **A**. Finally, use a 2-inch biscuit cutter to cut out an even smaller circle from each 4-inch round.

6. Carefully place an 8-inch vanilla cake ring on a cake plate. Place a 6-inch strawberry ring inside, followed by a 4-inch vanilla ring, then a 2-inch strawberry round **B**. Spread a thin layer of frosting on top **C**. (If cake feels too soft or begins to crumble, place in fridge to firm up.)

7. Place an 8-inch strawberry cake ring on top of first cake layer, then place a 6-inch vanilla ring inside, followed by a 4-inch strawberry ring, then a 2-inch vanilla round. Spread a thin layer of frosting on top.

8. Repeat steps 5 and 6 to make 4 layers total **B**.

9. Frost entire cake, then slice and serve.

WATCH & LEARN

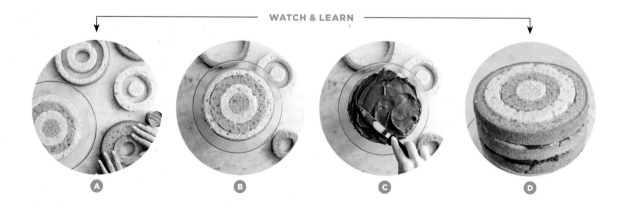

A   B   C   D

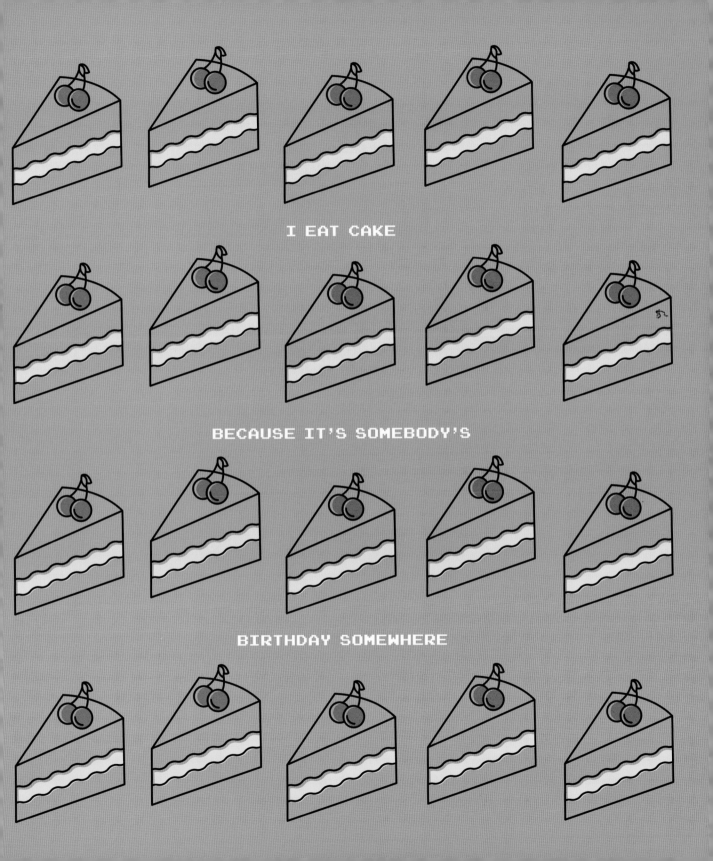

5 WAYS TO USE BROWNIE MIX

The boxed stuff can be used for so much more than you think.

1
HOT CHOCOLATE

In a small saucepan over medium heat, stir together ⅔ cup heavy cream, ½ cup brown sugar, ¼ cup brownie mix, ¼ cup corn syrup, 1 teaspoon pure vanilla extract, and ½ cup chocolate chips until melted. Stir in another ½ cup chocolate chips. Stir into mugs of warmed milk.

2
PANCAKES

Whisk together 1¼ cups brownie mix, 1 cup all-purpose flour, 1 teaspoon baking powder, 1 teaspoon baking soda, and ½ teaspoon kosher salt. Beat in 2 large eggs, 1 cup milk, and 1 teaspoon pure vanilla extract. Fold in ½ cup chocolate chips. Cook over medium heat in a greased nonstick skillet, 2 minutes per side.

3
ICE CREAM CUPS

Prepare 1 (18-ounce) box brownie mix according to box instructions. Grease a muffin tin with cooking spray. Pour brownie batter into prepared tin and bake at 350°F for 22 minutes. Use bottom of a shot glass to make a well in each brownie; let cool. Top with a scoop of ice cream.

4
BANANA BREAD

Stir together 1 (18-ounce) box brownie mix, 3 large eggs, and ½ cup melted butter. Stir in 2 mashed super-ripe bananas, ½ cup mini chocolate chips, and ¼ cup sour cream. Transfer to a greased loaf pan. Bake at 350°F until a toothpick comes out with very few crumbs attached, about 1 hour 10 minutes.

5
BROWNIE COOKIES

Stir together 1 (18-ounce) box brownie mix, 2 large eggs, ½ cup vegetable oil, and ¼ cup all-purpose flour. Fold in 1 cup chocolate chips. Roll dough into 1-inch balls and place on parchment-lined baking sheets. Bake at 350°F until just set, 12 minutes.

ROSÉ SORBET

TOTAL TIME: 1 HR 10 MIN / SERVES 6

We've been on the "rosé all day" train ever since we held a massive tasting at the office (serious research, people!) and had so many bottles to taste that we got a little too tipsy. You do need to make a rosé syrup for this (i.e., dump wine and sugar into a saucepan), but you don't need an ice cream maker, so you're still winning.

1 cup rosé wine

1¼ cups sugar

3 cups frozen raspberries

1. In a small saucepan over medium heat, combine rosé and sugar and bring to a boil, whisking constantly until sugar dissolves. Remove from heat and let rosé syrup cool to room temperature.

2. In a blender, combine frozen raspberries and ½ cup of rosé syrup and blend until smooth. Taste mixture, adding more rosé syrup if desired. (Store remaining syrup in the fridge up to one week.)

3. Pour into a 9x5-inch loaf pan, cover with plastic wrap, and freeze until firm, about 1 hour.

 This sorbet makes amazing BOOZY FLOATS: Scoop some into champagne flutes and top off with a splash of rosé, raspberries, and fresh mint.

SWISS ROLL CAKE

TOTAL TIME: 1 HR 15 MIN / SERVES 10 TO 12

Jo's greatest masterpiece at Delish. Little Debbie
knew how to do it right with that perfect cake-to-cream ratio.
For this, we filled a basic chocolate cake with marshmallow
frosting and studded the entire thing with sliced Swiss Rolls.
The end result is beautiful chaos.

Cooking spray

1 (15-ounce) box devil's
food cake mix, plus
ingredients called for
on box

**FOR THE
MARSHMALLOW
FILLING**

½ cup (1 stick) butter,
softened

1 cup powdered sugar

1 (7.5-ounce) jar
marshmallow creme

1 teaspoon pure vanilla
extract

FOR THE GANACHE

1½ cups chocolate chips

¾ cup heavy cream

24 Swiss Rolls, sliced
crosswise

1. Preheat oven to 350°F. Line two 8-inch round baking
pans with parchment paper and grease with cooking
spray.

2. Prepare cake mix according to box instructions.
Divide between prepared pans and bake until a
toothpick inserted into center of each cake comes
out clean, 30 minutes. Let cakes cool in pans for
10 minutes, then invert onto wire racks to cool
completely.

3. Make marshmallow filling: In a large bowl using a
hand mixer, beat butter, powdered sugar, marshmallow
creme, and vanilla until smooth and fluffy.

4. Make ganache: Put chocolate chips in a large
heatproof bowl. In a small saucepan over medium heat,
heat cream until steaming and bubbles form around
the edge. Pour over chocolate and let sit 5 minutes,
then whisk until completely melted and combined.

5. Assemble cake: Place one cake layer on a serving
platter. Spread marshmallow filling over cake and top
with second cake layer. Pour ganache over cake and
spread until entire cake is covered.

6. Apply Swiss Rolls in even rows around cake. Let set
30 minutes before slicing and serving.

BANANA SPLIT LASAGNA

TOTAL TIME: 4 HRS 35 MIN / SERVES 12 TO 14

We have reappropriated the word "lasagna" at Delish.
You don't need cheese—heck, you don't even need lasagna noodles—
to make one, just layers of deliciousness.

FOR THE CRUST

Cooking spray

2 cups crushed graham crackers

½ cup (1 stick) melted butter

2 tablespoons sugar

Pinch kosher salt

FOR THE LASAGNA

1½ (8-ounce) blocks cream cheese,
   softened

¼ cup sugar

2 (8-ounce) tubs Cool Whip

3 bananas, thinly sliced into rounds

1 (20-ounce) can crushed pineapple,
   well drained

1 pound strawberries, finely chopped

½ cup walnuts, toasted and chopped

Chocolate syrup, for drizzling

Rainbow sprinkles, for topping

Maraschino cherries, for topping

1. Make crust: Grease a 9x13-inch baking dish with cooking spray. In a medium bowl, stir together graham crackers, melted butter, sugar, and salt. Press into baking dish and refrigerate until set, 15 minutes.

2. In a large bowl using a hand mixer, beat cream cheese and sugar until light and fluffy, then fold in 1 tub Cool Whip. Spread mixture evenly onto crust.

3. Top cream layer with even layers of banana, pineapple, and strawberries. Top with remaining Cool Whip and sprinkle with walnuts.

4. Refrigerate at least 4 hours or up to overnight.

5. Drizzle with chocolate syrup and top with sprinkles and maraschino cherries before serving.

Minnie Dome Cake ⟶

DELISH GOES TO . . .
WALT DISNEY WORLD

Millions of people head to Walt Disney World each year for the insane attractions and to snag a photo with Mickey. We, on the other hand, are in it for the food. (And the booze.) The Delish team has been to Disney too many times to count, looking to celebrate—and document—the over-the-top treats they roll out every few months. (We also drank ourselves "around the world" at Epcot. Let's never mention it again.) It's safe to say that most Disney tourists don't even think about the amount of time and effort that goes into developing these treats—they're too busy Instagramming them—but there's a whole behind-the-scenes laboratory filled with geniuses bringing them to life. And while most might say this stuff looks too magical to eat—glow-in-the-dark drinks, candy apples the size of your head and decorated to the nines—that NEVER stops us.

Mickey Sugar ⟶
Cookie

Giant Turkey Leg

Character Caramel Apples ⟶

LeFou's Brew ⟶

Night Blossom

Banoffee Tart

Blueberry Cream
Cheese Mousse

Mickey Rice Crispy Cake

Mickey's
Kitchen Sink
Sundae

Mickey Pretzel

Mac & Cheese Hot Dog

Dole Whip Float

CHAPTER TWELVE

FRIENDSGIVING & MORE

CRANBERRY BRIE PULL-APART BREAD

TOTAL TIME: 35 MIN / SERVES 6

Just look at this thing. Cranberry Brie—it doesn't get more holiday than that—plus a stick of herb butter will make it the star of your spread.

1 large boule

½ cup (1 stick) melted butter

2 teaspoons fresh thyme leaves

2 teaspoons freshly chopped rosemary

Kosher salt

Freshly ground black pepper

1 (8-ounce) wheel Brie, cut into thin strips

1 (15-ounce) can whole-berry cranberry sauce

1. Preheat oven to 350°F and line a large baking sheet with parchment paper.

2. Using a serrated knife, crosshatch boule, slicing every inch in both directions and making sure not to slice all the way through the bottom.

3. In a small bowl, whisk together melted butter, thyme, and rosemary and season with salt and pepper. Brush boule with butter mixture, making sure to get inside crosshatches.

4. Stuff each crosshatch with Brie and cranberry sauce and wrap bread completely in foil.

5. Bake until cheese is melty and bread is warm and toasty, about 20 minutes.

6. Let cool 5 minutes, then serve.

IT'S A SNAP!   SLICE!   AGAIN!   STUFF!

When **CROSSHATCHING** the bread, slice as far down as you can without actually slicing through the bottom; you'll have a way easier time stuffing the ingredients inside.

CREAMED SPINACH STUFFED MUSHROOMS

TOTAL TIME: 35 MIN / SERVES 8

We're pretty sure we just turned a retro side into the most addictive holiday app ever. Mic drop.

2 pounds white mushrooms, stems removed

1 tablespoon extra-virgin olive oil

2 tablespoons butter

½ medium onion, finely chopped

3 cloves garlic, minced

½ (8-ounce) block cream cheese, softened

½ cup shredded mozzarella

Pinch ground nutmeg

Pinch cayenne pepper (optional)

Kosher salt

Freshly ground black pepper

1 (10-ounce) package frozen chopped spinach, thawed and squeezed of excess liquid

¼ cup freshly grated Parmesan

1. Preheat oven to 400°F.

2. On a large baking sheet, drizzle mushroom caps with oil and place stem-side down. Bake until mushrooms begin to shrink and release moisture, about 10 minutes.

3. Meanwhile, in a large skillet over medium heat, melt butter. Add onion and cook, stirring, until soft, 5 minutes. Add garlic and cook until fragrant, 1 minute. Add cream cheese, mozzarella, nutmeg, and cayenne (if using) and cook until cheese is melty. Season generously with salt and pepper and stir in chopped spinach. Remove from heat.

4. Flip over mushroom caps and stuff with spinach filling.

5. Bake until filling is golden and mushrooms are tender, about 15 minutes.

6. Sprinkle with Parmesan before serving.

CRANBERRY SHOTS

TOTAL TIME: 4 HRS / MAKES 18

Here's how to get really sauced on Friendsgiving: Hand these Jell-O shots out to your friends and don't look back.

1½ cups sugar, divided

1 cup fresh cranberries

2 (3.4-ounce) packets cranberry-flavored Jell-O

1 cup vodka

1. In a medium saucepan over medium heat, combine ½ cup of sugar and ½ cup water and stir until sugar dissolves completely. Let cool 20 minutes, then mix in cranberries until coated.

2. Using a slotted spoon, transfer cranberries, tapping away any excess syrup, into a large resealable plastic bag. Add remaining 1 cup sugar, seal, and shake until cranberries are completely coated.

3. Spread out cranberries on a baking sheet and refrigerate until cranberries are completely cool and sugar hardens, 25 minutes.

4. Bring 2 cups water to a boil. Add Jell-O mix and whisk until completely dissolved, then remove from heat and stir in vodka and 1 cup cold water. Let cool 2 to 3 minutes.

5. Place 18 plastic shot glasses on a baking sheet and pour in Jell-O mixture until each is ⅔ full.

6. Refrigerate until set, about 3 hours.

7. Top each shot with 1 or 2 sugared cranberries.

SWEET POTATO BITES

Casseroles are old school. This app has everything you love about the classic: gooey 'mallow and crunchy pecans in one bite.

3 to 4 medium sweet potatoes, peeled and sliced into ¼-inch-thick rounds

2 tablespoons melted butter

1 teaspoon maple syrup

Kosher salt

1 (10-ounce) bag marshmallows

½ cup pecan halves

1. Preheat oven to 400°F.

2. On a large baking sheet, toss sweet potatoes with melted butter and maple syrup and arrange in an even layer. Season with salt.

3. Bake until tender, flipping halfway through, about 20 minutes. Remove baking sheet from oven and switch oven to broil.

4. Top each sweet potato round with a marshmallow and broil until puffed and golden. Immediately top each marshmallow with a pecan half and serve.

GREEN BEAN CASSEROLE CUPS

TOTAL TIME: 40 MIN / MAKES 2 DOZEN

Whether you grew up on the mushy, gelatinous side or give it the side-eye, no one can deny that the crunch of fried onions and saltiness of cream of mushroom soup weirdly works. Serving them in crescent roll cups only makes them harder to hate.

Cooking spray

½ **pound green beans, trimmed and cut into ½-inch pieces**

1 **(10-ounce) can cream of mushroom soup**

1 **cup shredded white cheddar cheese**

1 **tablespoon Worcestershire sauce**

1 **teaspoon garlic powder**

Kosher salt

Freshly ground black pepper

All-purpose flour, for rolling

1 **(8-ounce) tube refrigerated crescent rolls, preferably sheets**

Crispy onions, for topping

1. Preheat oven to 375°F and grease a mini-muffin tin with cooking spray.

2. In a large bowl, stir together green beans, cream of mushroom soup, cheddar cheese, Worcestershire, and garlic powder and season generously with salt and pepper.

3. On a lightly floured surface, roll out crescent dough and cut into 24 squares. (If using rolls, pinch together perforated seams before cutting.) Place one square into each prepared muffin tin cup.

4. Spoon green bean mixture into crescent cups and sprinkle with crispy onions.

5. Bake until crescent pastry is golden, 12 to 15 minutes.

PICKLE-BRINED TURKEY

DELISH FAVE

TOTAL TIME: 12 HRS / SERVES 8 (WITH LEFTOVERS)

STOP YOUR HOLIDAY PLANNING. And put this on the menu. We can't stress enough how stupid-delicious this turkey is. The pickle juice won't make it taste sour (trust us on this one), but will make it the crispiest, prettiest turkey ever.

1 (12-pound) turkey, giblets removed

4 cups pickle juice

1 cup kosher salt

⅓ cup sugar

Freshly ground black pepper

2 lemons, halved

1 head garlic

1 onion, cut into wedges

1 bunch fresh dill

½ cup (1 stick) melted butter

1 teaspoon Old Bay seasoning

Pickle chips, for serving

 Serving on a bed of pickles is OPTIONAL, but why would you choose another way?!

1. Place turkey in a large pot and pour over pickle juice and 6 cups water. Add salt and sugar and season generously with pepper. Cover with plastic wrap and refrigerate 8 to 12 hours.

2. Preheat oven to 350°F with rack positioned in lower third.

3. Remove turkey from brine and rinse under cold water; pat dry with paper towels. Generously season turkey cavity with salt and pepper and stuff with lemons, garlic, onion, and dill.

4. In a small bowl, whisk together melted butter and Old Bay. Brush all over outside of turkey and season with salt and pepper.

5. Tie legs together with kitchen twine and tuck wing tips under body. Place turkey breast-side up on a roasting rack set inside a large roasting pan.

6. Bake turkey, basting every 45 minutes with pan juices, until the meat at the thigh registers 165°F, 3 to 4 hours.

7. Let rest 20 minutes before slicing. Serve over pickle chips.

THANKSGIVING CAULIFLOWER

TOTAL TIME: 1 HR 45 MIN / SERVES 4

"What if we roast a whole cauliflower like a chicken?" Jo posed to Lauren a while back. Then it hit us: Thanksgiving. Instead of chicken, we basted the cauliflower head with butter like it was a giant turkey. Your vegetarian guests will lose their minds.

1 large head cauliflower

4 tablespoons melted butter, divided

Kosher salt

Freshly ground black pepper

4 whole cloves garlic (skin-on)

4 leaves fresh sage

4 sprigs fresh thyme

4 sprigs fresh rosemary

FOR THE GRAVY

4 tablespoons butter

½ onion, finely chopped

4 ounces cremini mushrooms, finely chopped

1 teaspoon freshly chopped sage

1 teaspoon freshly chopped rosemary

1 teaspoon freshly chopped thyme

3 tablespoons all-purpose flour

2 to 4 cups low-sodium vegetable broth

1. Preheat oven to 450°F.

2. Put cauliflower in a large oven-safe skillet, rub all over with 2 tablespoons of melted butter, and season with salt and pepper. Arrange garlic and herbs around cauliflower.

3. Bake until cauliflower is tender and slightly charred, brushing with remaining 2 tablespoons melted butter halfway through, 1 hour to 1 hour 30 minutes. (Pierce cauliflower with a paring knife to check if it's ready.)

4. Make gravy: In a small saucepan over medium heat, melt butter. Add onion and cook, stirring until soft, 5 minutes. Stir in mushrooms and herbs and season with salt and pepper. Cook, stirring, until mushrooms are soft and golden, about 4 minutes. Add 1 or 2 cloves of the roasted garlic (skins removed), breaking up cloves with a wooden spoon. Stir in flour and cook 1 minute, then whisk in 2 cups of broth and bring mixture to a boil. Reduce heat to low and simmer until mixture has thickened to your desired consistency, 5 minutes. (Add more broth if desired.)

5. Serve cauliflower with gravy.

The
**ROASTED
GARLIC
GRAVY**
is the real
winner here.

ONION SOUP
STANDING RIB ROAST

TOTAL TIME: 2 HRS 25 MIN / SERVES 10 TO 12

The same packet that transforms sour cream into the world's most amazing chip dip turns a standing rib roast—the most majestic of roasts—into something insanely flavorful. As the drippings fall off the meat while it cooks, they mix with the spices and create something out of this world.

1 (8-pound) standing rib roast

1 (1-ounce) packet onion soup mix, such as Lipton Recipe Secrets

1. Preheat oven to 450°F.

2. Let beef come to room temperature as oven preheats. Season beef with onion soup mix, making sure to cover all exposed sides, and place in a roasting pan, fattiest-side up.

3. Roast 15 minutes to sear the outside, then reduce oven temperature to 350°F and cook until meat is medium-rare and internal temperature reads 120°F when taken with a meat thermometer, about 2 hours (15 minutes per pound).

4. Drape meat with foil and let rest 10 minutes before slicing.

CHEESE-STUFFED CORNBREAD

TOTAL TIME: 45 MIN / SERVES 8

'Tis the season for cheese, cheese, and more cheese.
To ensure melty pepper jack in every bite, we add it cubed instead
of grated, which makes for an epic cheese pull.

½ cup (1 stick) melted butter, plus more for skillet

1 cup buttermilk

¼ cup honey

2 large eggs

1 cup all-purpose flour

1 cup yellow cornmeal

2½ teaspoons baking powder

¼ teaspoon kosher salt

6 ounces pepper jack cheese, cubed

Freshly chopped chives, for garnish

1. Preheat oven to 375°F and butter a 10- or 12-inch oven-safe skillet.

2. In a medium bowl, whisk together buttermilk, melted butter, honey, and eggs until combined.

3. In a large bowl, whisk together flour, cornmeal, baking powder, and salt. Pour wet ingredients over dry and stir until just combined.

4. Spread half the cornbread batter into prepared skillet and scatter pepper jack cheese over batter in an even layer. Pour over remaining batter, spreading it to cover cheese.

5. Bake until golden and cooked through, 25 to 30 minutes.

6. Let cool 5 minutes in skillet, then garnish with chives and cut into squares.

CHEESY BRUSSELS SPROUT BAKE

TOTAL TIME: 35 MIN / SERVES 6

When we shot this picture, Lauren and Lindsay stood over the pan and finished off the entire thing to themselves—at ten in the morning. We all know Brussels sprouts and bacon are made for each other; add sharp cheddar and cream, and it's serious trouble.

5 slices bacon

3 tablespoons butter

2 small shallots, minced

2 pounds Brussels sprouts, halved

Kosher salt

½ teaspoon cayenne pepper

¾ cup heavy cream

½ cup shredded sharp white cheddar cheese

½ cup shredded Gruyère cheese

1. Preheat oven to 375°F.

2. In a large oven-safe skillet over medium heat, cook bacon until crispy, 8 minutes. Drain on a paper towel-lined plate, then chop. Discard bacon fat.

3. Return skillet to medium heat and melt butter. Add shallots and Brussels sprouts and season with salt and cayenne. Cook, stirring occasionally, until tender, about 10 minutes.

4. Remove from heat and drizzle with heavy cream, then top with both cheeses and bacon.

5. Bake until cheese is bubbly, 12 to 15 minutes. (If your cheese isn't golden, switch oven to broil and broil 1 minute.)

BEER CHEESE STUFFING

TOTAL TIME: 1 HR 20 MIN / SERVES 8

This will make you seriously question why we only eat stuffing at Thanksgiving (but seriously, WHY?!). Beer + cheddar + bacon is the side that demands seconds.

2 tablespoons butter, cut into ½-inch pieces, plus more for baking dish

8 slices bacon

1 large onion, finely chopped

4 stalks celery, finely chopped

Kosher salt

Freshly ground black pepper

½ cup medium-bodied beer, such as an IPA

10 cups cubed French bread, dried overnight

1 cup shredded sharp white cheddar cheese, divided

1 tablespoon fresh thyme leaves

2 cups low-sodium chicken broth

1 teaspoon Worcestershire sauce

2 large eggs, beaten

Freshly chopped parsley, for garnish

1. Preheat oven to 425°F and butter a 3-quart baking dish.

2. In a large skillet over medium heat, cook bacon until crispy, about 8 minutes. Drain on a paper towel–lined plate, then chop.

3. Add onion and celery to bacon fat in skillet and season with salt and pepper. Cook until soft, about 5 minutes. Add beer and simmer, scraping up any browned bits from bottom of pan, until almost evaporated, about 2 minutes. Add bread, ⅔ cup of cheddar cheese, thyme, and half of cooked bacon and toss to combine.

4. Add broth, Worcestershire, and eggs and toss to combine.

5. Scatter stuffing with remaining ⅓ cup cheddar cheese and cooked bacon and cover with foil. Bake until a knife inserted into center comes out warm, 45 minutes.

6. Let rest 10 minutes, then garnish with parsley before serving.

GARLIC SMASHED POTATOES

TOTAL TIME: 55 MIN / SERVES 4

Smashed > mashed. People lost their minds over these roasted potatoes because of the surprising (and weirdly stress-relieving) smashing technique, but it's the texture that will really get you: ultra-crispy on the outside, ultra-creamy on the inside.

1½ pounds baby Yukon Gold potatoes

Kosher salt

4 tablespoons melted butter

2 cloves garlic, minced

1 teaspoon fresh thyme leaves

Freshly ground black pepper

½ cup freshly grated Parmesan

1. Preheat oven to 425°F.

2. In a large pot, cover potatoes with water and add a generous pinch of salt. Bring water to a boil and simmer until potatoes are tender, about 15 minutes. Drain and let sit until cool enough to handle.

3. On a large rimmed baking sheet, toss potatoes with melted butter, garlic, and thyme. Using bottom of a small glass or mason jar, press down on potatoes to smash them into flat patties.

4. Season with salt and pepper, then sprinkle with Parmesan.

5. Bake until bottoms of potatoes are beginning to crisp and Parmesan is golden, about 25 minutes.

You can top these with more than just Parm. Try BACON and CHEDDAR, RANCH seasoning, or BRIE.

THANKSGIVING RING

TOTAL TIME: 30 MIN / SERVES 8

Thanksgiving leftovers aren't regular leftovers—they're *cool* leftovers. Regular leftovers get pushed to the back of the fridge; Thanksgiving ones get demolished immediately when transformed into this masterpiece.

1 (8-ounce) tube crescent rolls

1 cup leftover mashed potatoes

1 cup leftover stuffing

1½ cups shredded leftover turkey

1 cup leftover cranberry sauce

1 tablespoon melted butter

1 tablespoon garlic powder

Freshly chopped parsley, for garnish

Leftover gravy, warmed, for dipping

1. Preheat oven to 375°F.

2. Unroll crescent rolls, separating each triangle. Arrange on baking sheet in a sunburst pattern, with pointy ends of triangles facing outward and bases of triangles overlapping.

3. Spread mashed potatoes over triangle bases, forming a ring. Top with stuffing, turkey, and cranberry sauce. Fold triangle tips over filling (there will be gaps where ingredients peek out between triangles).

4. Brush crescent dough with melted butter and sprinkle with garlic powder.

5. Bake until golden, 15 to 20 minutes.

6. Garnish with parsley and serve with gravy for dipping.

GOBBLE-GOBBLE, INDEED.

PUMPKIN CHEESECAKE LASAGNA

TOTAL TIME: 4 HRS 30 MIN / SERVES 12 TO 15

This dessert is like pumpkin pie and cheesecake had a baby. Get ready—your Thanksgiving guests will demand it forever more.

1 (8-ounce) block cream cheese, softened

¼ cup sugar

½ cup heavy cream

2 cups whole milk

3 (3.4-ounce) packages vanilla pudding mix

1 cup pumpkin puree

1 teaspoon pumpkin pie spice

12 graham cracker sheets

¼ cup caramel

Chopped pecans, for garnish

1. In a large bowl using a hand mixer or in the bowl of stand mixer using the whisk attachment, beat cream cheese and sugar until light and fluffy. Slowly add heavy cream and beat until stiff peaks form.

2. In a medium bowl, whisk together milk, pudding mix, pumpkin, and pumpkin pie spice until smooth and thick.

3. Assemble lasagna: Spread a thin layer of cream cheese mixture in a 9x13-inch baking dish. Top with a layer of six graham crackers. Add half of pudding mixture and top with half of cream cheese mixture. Drizzle with half of caramel and repeat, ending with cream cheese layer (reserve remaining caramel until ready to serve).

4. Cover loosely with plastic wrap and refrigerate at least 4 hours and up to overnight.

5. Drizzle with remaining caramel and garnish with pecans before serving.

THANKSGIVING CAKE

BREE'S CAKES / Los Angeles, CA

Forget Turduckens and Cherpumples: The latest in over-the-top, Frankenstein-ish Turkey Day dishes is an entire meal . . . in cake form. Bree Miller of Bree's Cakes, a Los Angeles–based bakery, broke the Internet when she created a fried chicken and mashed potato cake. Within five minutes of her posting a photo of the cake to Instagram, The Game's assistant called her: The rapper wanted three cakes to serve at Thanksgiving dinner. Before long, Kevin Hart and Chrissy Teigen placed orders, too. Naturally, we wanted in, and turned to Miller with a mission: Create an even wilder confection based entirely on Thanksgiving classics. Miller returned with towering layers of cornbread, stuffing, and sweet potato casserole, frosted and piped with mashed potatoes. The whole thing's crowned with a whole roasted Cornish hen, meant to look like a little turkey on top of the cake. "Building the cake took no time—but prepping out and making every dish that goes into it can take quite a few hours," she admits. "But the reaction it gets is worth it."

GINGERBREAD EGGNOG

TOTAL TIME: 10 MIN / SERVES 4

It's not Christmas without a boozy eggnog. Molasses might seem like an odd addition here, but it adds a smoky, slightly spicy sweetness to the whole experience.

1 tablespoon cinnamon sugar

Ice

1 cup eggnog

1 cup vodka

1 cup Kahlúa

2 tablespoons molasses, plus more for drizzling

Pinch ground ginger

Whipped cream, for topping

1. Wet rims of four cocktail glasses and dip in cinnamon sugar.

2. In a cocktail shaker filled with ice, add eggnog, vodka, Kahlúa, molasses, and ginger and shake to combine.

3. Pour into rimmed glasses. Top with whipped cream and drizzle with molasses before serving.

COOKIE BUTTER CHEESECAKE

TOTAL TIME: 7 HRS / SERVES 10 TO 12

We eat cookie butter straight from the jar with a spoon.
Made from the crumbs of spiced shortbread cookies, it's got all the flavors—
cinnamon, ginger, nutmeg—that taste like Christmas.

FOR THE CRUST

¼ cup (½ stick) melted butter, plus more for pan

30 Speculoos or Biscoff cookies

⅛ teaspoon kosher salt

FOR THE CHEESECAKE

4 (8-ounce) blocks cream cheese, softened

1¼ cups sugar

½ teaspoon kosher salt

4 large eggs

1 cup heavy cream

¼ cup sour cream

1 tablespoon pure vanilla extract

½ cup cookie butter

5 Speculoos or Biscoff cookies, crushed, for garnish

½ cup cookie butter, melted, for garnish

1. Make crust: Set a rack in middle of oven and preheat to 350°F. Butter a 9-inch springform pan and wrap bottom and sides of pan in a double layer of aluminum foil.

2. In a food processor or blender, grind cookies into fine crumbs. Add salt and pulse to combine. Transfer to a medium bowl, add melted butter, and use a fork or your fingers to blend until crumbs are evenly moistened. Press into bottom and about ⅓ up sides of prepared pan.

3. Place pan on baking sheet and bake crust for 10 minutes. Transfer to a wire rack to cool. Reduce oven temperature to 325°F.

4. Make cheesecake: In a large bowl using a hand mixer, or in bowl of a stand mixer using paddle attachment, beat cream cheese until completely smooth, 3 minutes. Add sugar and salt and beat until smooth and fluffy, 2 minutes more. Add eggs, one at a time, beating after each addition and scraping down bowl as necessary. Add heavy cream, sour cream, and vanilla and beat until fully incorporated, 1 minute. Gently fold in cookie butter. Pour cheesecake batter into cooled crust and smooth top.

RECIPE CONTINUES

5. Bring a medium saucepan full of water to a boil. Place cheesecake in a deep roasting pan and set on middle rack of oven. Carefully pour enough boiling water into roasting pan to come halfway up sides of springform pan. Bake until cheesecake is just starting to brown and only the center is slightly jiggly, 1 hour 20 minutes. Turn off oven, prop open door with a wooden spoon, and let cheesecake slowly cool in water bath, 1 hour.

6. Remove roasting pan from oven, then carefully lift springform pan from water and remove foil. Set cheesecake on a rack and let come to room temperature. Once completely cool, loosely cover with plastic wrap and refrigerate until firm, 4 hours or up to overnight.

7. When ready to serve, carefully unmold from springform pan. Sprinkle cheesecake top with crushed cookies and drizzle with melted cookie butter.

 FYI: You can find SPECULOOS COOKIES at Trader Joe's, World Market, and other specialty supermarkets. They're worth every penny.

ANDES LAYER CAKE

TOTAL TIME: 1 HR 30 MIN / SERVES 10 TO 12

If we had to choose between being single or eating this peppermint buttercream every day for the rest of our lives, we might choose the buttercream. (Selfish, we know).

FOR THE CAKE
Cooking spray

3½ cups all-purpose flour

3½ cups sugar

1½ cups cocoa powder

2 teaspoons baking powder

1 teaspoon baking soda

2 teaspoons kosher salt

2 cups buttermilk

1 cup vegetable oil

4 large eggs

1½ teaspoons pure vanilla extract

FOR THE GANACHE

1 cup heavy cream

1 cup semisweet chocolate chips

FOR THE PEPPERMINT BUTTERCREAM

3 cups powdered sugar

1 cup butter, softened

2 tablespoons whole milk

1 teaspoon peppermint extract

4 to 6 drops green gel food coloring

1 (4-ounce) box Andes mints, chopped

1. Preheat oven to 350°F. Line three 9-inch round cake pans with parchment and grease with cooking spray.

2. In a large bowl, whisk together flour, sugar, cocoa powder, baking powder, baking soda, and salt.

3. In a small saucepan, bring 2 cups water to a boil, then remove from heat.

4. In another large bowl using a hand mixer, beat buttermilk, oil, eggs, and vanilla until combined. Add dry ingredients alternately with the hot water in batches and beat until well combined.

5. Divide batter among prepared pans. Bake until a toothpick inserted into center of each cake comes out clean, 35 to 40 minutes. Let cakes cool for 10 minutes, then invert onto wire racks to cool completely.

6. Meanwhile, make ganache: Put chocolate chips in a large heatproof bowl. In a small saucepan over medium heat, heat cream until steaming and bubbles form around the edge. Pour cream over chocolate and let sit 5 minutes, then whisk until completely melted and combined. Let cool slightly.

7. Make buttercream: In a large bowl using a hand mixer, beat powdered sugar, butter, milk, and peppermint extract until light and fluffy. Stir in food coloring.

8. On a serving platter, layer cakes and buttercream. Pour over ganache and top with Andes.

CONFETTI COOKIE DOUGH BALL

TOTAL TIME: 3 HRS 15 MIN / SERVES 10 TO 12

Just like a dessert cheese ball. This (flour-free!) cookie dough tastes just like the real thing—and is definitely the only ball your friends are gonna care about on New Year's Eve.

1½ (8-ounce) blocks cream cheese, softened

4 tablespoons (½ stick) butter, softened

½ cup powdered sugar

¼ cup packed brown sugar

½ teaspoon pure vanilla extract

1 cup mini chocolate chips

¾ cup assorted rainbow and silver sprinkles

Nilla wafers and pretzels, for serving

1. In a large bowl using a hand mixer, beat cream cheese and butter until light and fluffy. Beat in powdered sugar, brown sugar, and vanilla, then fold in chocolate chips.

2. Place two overlapping sheets of plastic wrap on a work surface and scrape cookie dough mixture on top. Using your hands, form mixture into a ball. Place in a small bowl, then cover tightly with plastic and refrigerate until firm, 3 hours. (Once it's semi-firm, after 2 hours, you'll be able to better shape it into a ball.)

3. In a small bowl, mix together rainbow and silver sprinkles.

4. When ready to serve, transfer ball to a serving platter and cover entirely with sprinkles. (If your ball is firm enough to roll, try that.)

5. Serve with Nilla wafers and pretzels.

ACKNOWLEDGMENTS

A HUGE THANK-YOU

• • •

To **Lindsay Funston**, who not only helped build this book out of nothing, but also helped build this brand out of nothing. She is never afraid to challenge the popular view, and her constant drive to understand, guide, and serve our readers kills me every single day. Thank you also to **Jesse**, who literally gave her up for four months while she made this book.

To **Lindsey Ramsey**, my rock, my muscle, my goalie. There is no feat she can't handle, no problem she can't solve, and no sentence of mine she can't . . . wait, let me read this email. This book would not be in your hands right now without her.

To **Lauren Miyashiro**, whose passion and enthusiasm is the secret ingredient to nearly every recipe in here; she gave everything for this book, and I am beyond lucky to have her. And to **Lena Abraham**, **Makinze Gore**, **Alyssa Rosello**, **June (Jiuxing) Xie**, and **Rian Handler**, who made sure that every single thing comes out perfectly.

To **Nick Neubeck,** work husband and unpaid therapist. He is our Ron Howard—the creative glue that holds this brand (and this book) together—and he always turns every insane, random, and chaotic idea we drop at his feet into something extraordinary.

To **Candace Braun** and **Sarah Weinberg**, who worked tirelessly to hunt down the fun stories, restaurants, and excursions crammed into these pages. Lord knows they've sacrificed their pride for their content, but they never sacrifice quality, and I am beyond grateful for both of them.

To **Ethan Calabrese**, photographer and staff little brother. We might complain about his music choices, but our food looks infinitely better through his lens, and he always knows when to make us reel it in.

To **Katja Cho** and **Allie Folino**, who produced the incredible graphics and icons seen throughout these pages. If Delish were a language, they would undoubtedly be its alphabet. To **Jessica Musumeci**, who conceived and executed this amazing cover . . . and so much more over the years.

To the **entire Delish team**, for the hard work they do every day to make so many people in the world happy, and the work they do to make sure no one leaves hungry.

To **Kate Lewis**, who went out on a limb and trusted me with this brand. She is our loudest cheerleader, and she pushes us to be better every day. And to **Troy Young**, who gives us all the guidance and resources, keeps us on our toes, and loves to complain about how trashy our food is while simultaneously stuffing his face.

To **Jacqueline Deval**, for taking my meeting and making this book a reality. And to **Justin Schwartz**, **Melissa Lotfy**, **Marina Padakis Lowry**, and everyone at **Houghton Mifflin Harcourt**, who have been incredibly supportive throughout this process, and who never judged us when we were like, "So how do you make a book?" And finally, to our designer, **Laura Palese**, who transformed our madness into magic.

To my husband, **Scott**, my absolute North Star, for believing in me long before I believed in myself. To my parents, **Barbara** and **Joe**, who taught me that life is really just a series of excuses to throw a great party. To my sister, **Laura**, who inspires me every day to eyeball it. And to my children, **Spencer**, **Teddy**, and **Everett**, for bringing me endless happiness and pride every single day. All I can hope is that one day they'll know what it feels like to truly love what you do.

INDEX

Page references in *italics* indicate photographs.

CREDITS

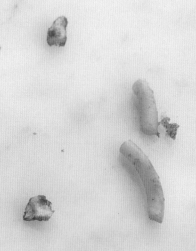